16049. +2⁵⁰   40—

Wlam

SO-ABB-116

Against Islamic Extremism

University Press of Florida

Gainesville · Tallahassee · Tampa · Boca Raton · Pensacola · Orlando · Miami · Jacksonville

Against
Islamic
Extremism

The Writings of Muhammad Sa'id al-'Ashmawy

Edited by Carolyn Fluehr-Lobban

03   02   01   00   99   98   6   5   4   3   2   1

Library of Congress Cataloging-in-Publication Data
Ashmāwī, Muhammad Sa'īd.
Against Islamic Extremism: the writings of Muhammad Sa'id
al-'Ashmawy / edited by Carolyn Fluehr-Lobban.
p. cm.
Includes bibliographical references (p.).
ISBN 0–8130–1546–4 (alk. paper)
1. Islamic fundamentalism. 2. Islam—20th century.
I. Fluehr-Lobban, Carolyn. II. Title.
BP60.A8 1998
297.2'72—dc21   97–24411

The University Press of Florida is the scholarly publishing agency for
the State University System of Florida, comprised of Florida A&M
University, Florida Atlantic University, Florida International University,
Florida State University, University of Central Florida, University of
Florida, University of North Florida, University of South Florida, and
University of West Florida.

University Press of Florida
15 Northwest 15th Street
Gainesville, Florida 32611
http: //nersp.nerdc.ufl.edu/~upf

Contents

Acknowledgments

First and foremost I gratefully acknowledge the interest and cooperation of Muhammad Sa'id al-'Ashmawy in this collaborative effort to bring out a first comprehensive book of his writings in English. A previous work, *Islam and the Political Order* (1994) is a translation from the French of an original work in Arabic, *Al-Islam al-Siyasi* (Political Islam), published in 1987. The present volume is the first work to pull together a broad selection of Dr. al-'Ashmawy's writings and lectures taken from the past turbulent decade, with Dr. al-'Ashmawy as an active collaborator. His writings were initially a response to the growing Islamist trend in Egypt, many of the events of which he experienced firsthand as a leading figure in the judiciary. However, Muhammad Sa'id al-'Ashmawy has grown to be a leading international figure in the scholarly and intellectual struggle against Islamic extremism, a battle requiring great courage in these times. Without the intellectual and spiritual vision that al-'Ashmawy expresses in these pages, we would not have such a powerful voice raised for humanism in Islam and as a response to the crises and challenges that characterize the Middle East region today.

Second, I gratefully acknowledge the critical assistance of the Rhode Island College Faculty Research Fund, which has generously supported the editing and typing of this manuscript. The articles in this book have been culled from a large number of diverse sources. In this regard, I am especially grateful to Gita Brown, whose expert editing skills and talent for developing logical flow in the text have been invaluable.

The entire text has been read, revised, and approved by Muhammad Sa'id al-'Ashmawy. My suggestions to improve language or phrasing in the text have been made explicit, as was my request to respond to the specific issues of human rights and women's rights. Standard Arabic transliteration has been employed throughout the text. The glossary of terms was derived from the introduction and text and compiled by Dr. al-'Ashmawy and me.

Introducing Muhammad Sa'id al-'Ashmawy
to an English-Language Audience

Muhammad Sa'id al-'Ashmawy, former chief justice of the High Court of Cairo, has emerged since his retirement as one of Egypt's leading intellectual secularist voices and a leading opponent of the Islamist political trend. He has gained recognition throughout the Arabic-speaking world as a jurist, religious scholar, and intellectual who opposes extremist political activism in the name of Islam. He has become a leader among the many voices of intellectuals, jurists, and scholars who have confronted the politicizing of Islam, using it to justify violence as a political tool. His writings are not so much a direct response to the militants' ideology (because he finds much that is flawed in their thinking), but they are very much a response to the harm being done to Islam as a faith, for which he believes the militants to be responsible.

Unfortunately, we read and hear too little of this critical Muslim point of view in the Western media. Figures such as Dr. al-'Ashmawy who have courageously made themselves available to the regional and international press tend to gain recognition after some attack is perpetrated against them or they have actually been assassinated, as was Egyptian journalist Farag Foda. The Islamist-inspired assault on the Nobel Laureate writer Naguib Mahfouz was both a shock and a wake-up call to Egyptian intellectuals and writers of any orientation who are judged not to conform to a narrow Islamist agenda. Outraged by such attacks, Dr. al-ʿAshmawy has declined opportunities to live or work abroad, choosing instead to remain in Egypt although he has been threatened by Islamist extremists. He currently lives under twenty-four-hour armed guard at his apartment in Cairo.

Western media attention has more often focused on the Islamist leaders, who are perceived as threats to the West and its interests in the Middle East, than on the voices of opposition to these tendencies. Lengthy interviews in the English-language press with fundamentalist leaders like Hasan al-Turābī of the Sudan, or Rashid al-Ghanoushī of Tunisia in the French press, are more likely to be covered than are interviews with those who might critique their approach, like Dr. al-ʿAshmawy. Criticism of Islamist extremism may be more likely to be heard from the subjective, literary viewpoint of a writer like Salman Rushdie than from qualified Muslim jurists, scholars, and writers, such as Muhammad Saʿid al-ʿAshmawy. Leading Western experts on Islam repeatedly call for an appreciation of the differences among those we label "Islamic fundamentalists" and caution against overestimating the "Islamic threat" (Esposito 1992; Halliday 1996).

Muhammad Saʿid al-ʿAshmawy is one of the most frequently quoted Egyptian writers; his comments on regional affairs are regularly cited in the Western press, including that of the United States. He commented extensively on the trial of Sheikh ʿOmer ʿAbdel Rahman, in which he spoke of his fears of the likelihood of retaliation by militant Islamists (*New York Times*, October 2, 1995). He was strongly and openly critical of a 1995 Egyptian Appeals Court decision in a case that imposed "divorce for apostasy" upon Cairo University Professor Nasr Abu Zeid, declaring him an apostate from Islam for his writings. In this case, which received a great deal of attention in the West as well as in the Middle East, Professor Zeid's doctoral thesis was judged by Islamist evaluators to be "anti-Islamist"; as a result, the court determined that an apostate could not be married to a Muslim woman, so the couple had to be separated. In a press interview that circulated on the Internet, Dr. al-ʿAshmawy said that "this ruling is very dangerous; it will simply encourage people to file lawsuits against any writer or intellectual who dares to speak out against the extremists. These extremists, he argued, have infiltrated the judiciary, the government knows it and has done very little to stop it. I doubt that the judiciary is neutral anymore" (COMPASS Newswire, June 15, 1995). This statement is significant; it not only criticizes the extremist interpretation of Islamic family law that separated a man and wife without their mutual consent but is also critical of the state judiciary that has capitulated to this degree to Islamist views. The couple currently live in exile, ouside of Egypt.

Trained as a specialist in Islamic law and comparative law, Muhammad Saʿid al-ʿAshmawy earned his law degree from Cairo University in 1954 and began his legal career as assistant district attorney in Alexandria, serving there until the early 1960s. In 1961 he was appointed to the position of judge, and in 1971 he was elevated to chief prosecutor. In 1981 he was made chief justice of the High Criminal Court, as well as chief justice of the High Court of Assizes and chief justice of the High Court for Security of State. During these years, as he rose to the highest levels of the Egyptian legal system, Muhammad Saʿid al-ʿAshmawy began his extra-judicial writing, publishing numerous works in Arabic and lecturing widely in Europe, Africa, Asia, and North America. Given his extensive government service, his public statements about the aforementioned apostasy case are all the more striking and significant.

This collection is a unique synthesis of al-ʿAshmawy's writings originally drafted for scholarly lectures presented in Europe, the United States, Canada, India, and in the Middle East. Over the years he sent me copies of his lectures, and in 1994 we agreed that a unified volume of his work in English would be a good idea. This volume was created from writings that either were originally written and delivered in English (at Harvard University or in Salzburg, Austria, for example) or were written in Arabic and translated by Muhammad Saʿid al-ʿAshmawy. Together with writer-editor Gita Brown of Providence we created this volume, which systematizes al-ʿAshmawy's thought on the subject of humanism in Islam as a tool against Islamic extremism.

Dr. al-ʿAshmawy and I met for the first time in 1983 at the American University in Cairo where we appeared on a panel addressing issues of Islamic law in contemporary society. He had never heard a Westerner speak as favorably as I did about Islamic family law, and I was struck by his liberal and humanistic approach to the religion and law of Islam. This collection of his writings is offered in order to provide a Western audience with the opportunity to hear authoritative yet critical voices from the Middle East at a time when the region is facing its greatest intellectual challenge in decades.

The threats against al-ʿAshmawy began in 1979 after the publication of *Usul al-Sharīʿa* (Roots of Islamic law), which launched his career in Egypt as an unconventional and provocative juristic thinker. He has been under continuous government protection since 1980, for thirteen years while still in government service and since his retirement in 1993. In 1992 there was an attempt by sheikhs from al-Azhar Islamic University to have al-ʿAshmawy's books banned at the popular annual Cairo International Book Fair. However, since he was still chief justice, the Egyptian government intervened (President Hosni Mubarak himself) and prevented the banning. His books are available in Egypt as well as his writings that appear on a regular basis in the Arabic press, especially *October Magazine.*

Introduction to Humanism in Islam

The term *Islamic* has been attached to multiple nouns and descriptions of current events in the Middle East—"Islamic fundamentalism," "Islamic militants," "Islamic extremists," "Islamic resurgence or revival"— but the term *humanism* in association with Islam has rarely been employed by a contemporary Muslim author until this work. Humanism is a world view that we are accustomed to attributing to Western thought and traditions, a product of European enlightenment. Humanism, with its focus on human beings, may even appear to be inconsistent with religion's focus on God, God's word, and God's commands. However, humanism has profoundly affected Christianity and Judaism, as well as Islam, especially with the deeply mystical (Sūfī) traditions. And contemporary mainstream Islam may be in the midst of a period of review, enlightenment, and renaissance as an outcome of nineteenth- and twentieth-century struggles for direction in every Muslim nation.

Humanistic thinking is pervasive among the contemporary writers who challenge Islamic conservative, retrogressive thought; thus we situate humanism as a concept within an Islamic framework using the writings of Muhammad Saʿid al-ʿAshmawy. Unlike "secular humanism," which has been accused in the West of being antireligious, Islamic humanism combines the use of the human power of reasoning with a universal religious spirit of the oneness of God and the oneness and unity of humanity.

By probing the foundations of belief in multiple religious traditions as shown in the selections in this book, al-ʿAshmawy reveals a common human spiritual core revealing a clearly universal humanism. He traces to the great Egyptian teacher Osiris the origin of this one religion and one message of God, which, although expressed by a "symbolic polytheism," was nevertheless the concept of the one infinite and eternal God, who was without rival. Thus, for al-ʿAshmawy, Egyptian monotheistic beliefs preceded but prepared the way for the monotheistic path forged by Judaism, Christianity, and Islam. Moreover, the moral and jural systems created by these faiths were extensions of the religious charter for living laid down by the ancient Egyptians. Part I of this book, "Islam, Judaism, Christianity: One Religion, One Vision, Many Paths," shows the unified development of religion as a single river into which many streams have flowed. Humanism is one expression of this universal message.

Muhammad Saʿid al-ʿAshmawy sees a critical need for the creation of a new politics in the Middle East fashioned from a humanist vision that would embrace the region's multiple social and religious traditions. He envisions a humanism based on Islamic faith and the other great faiths that have emanated from the Middle East. To conceive of a unique Islamic humanism, in the strictest sense, belies the fact that humanism is a universal philosophy embracing all of humanity, irrespective of language, nation, ethnicity, gender, class, race, or religion. Thus, Al-'Ashmawy's vision of Islam is not for Muslims alone but for all humanity.

On a personal note, during one of my visits with Sa'id al-'Ashmawy in 1995, at the time of the Coptic Christmas holiday, he was busy calling numerous Christian leaders to convey his holiday and New Year greetings. He has repeatedly spoken out against alleged government discrimination against Christians and the Coptic Church. He has criticized the 139-year-old edict that makes necessary a presidential decree to build or rebuild a church and that church construction must pass a ten-step review, including an evaluation of the impact on nearby irrigation canals, railroads, and Muslim neighborhoods. On the other hand, construction of a mosque requires only a simple engineering license, al-'Ashmawy noted in a recent interview, along with the fact that about 30,000 new mosques have been built since 1970 without any approval at all (*Philadelphia Inquirer*, June 23, 1995).

In the humanistic view, there is no punishing or vengeful God; the notion of a vengeful God is not appropriate to this era in human history, according to al-'Ashmawy. In order for religion to survive and to thrive, it must be returned to the hands of the people. Historically, it has been the case that institutionalized religion abandoned the people of all the faiths, not the other way around. Al-'Ashmawy defines one ethical and moral code for all human beings—to be upright in conduct. No people of any faith that follows this moral code should be excluded on any grounds. It is here that al-'Ashmawy differs so fundamentally from Islamic extremists. The extremists believe that the message of God, revealed to the Prophet Muhammad, was for Muslims exclusively. The popular Sūfī mystical tradition in Islam has always had a more universalist, open, and humanist approach that has favored inclusion rather than exclusion with respect to belief and practice. At its philosophical core Sufism is deeply humanistic, but—unlike the experience of a thinker such as Sa'id al-

'Ashmawy, whose entire career has been associated with the state and with urban life—the Sūfīs, whom many argue represent the heart and soul of Islam, have existed at the fringes of official Islam and the state. What makes al-'Ashmawy's writings all the more remarkable is their humanistic core, despite a lengthy political experience that might have made him more cynical than humanist.

The Islamist exclusionary view harkens back to the notion of the division of the world into *Dār al-Islām* (the abode of Muslims) and *Dār al-Harb* (the abode of non-Muslims, of war). Historically, this bipolar worldview has justified both expansionistic and defensive *jihād* (war), and a number of extremist movements have used the concept of jihād as a mobilizing tool. Al-'Ashmawy believes that such a division is no longer appropriate in today's world and should be supplanted by humanistic interpretations of Islam that acknowledge the multiple religious heritages that co-exist with Islam.

A humanistic approach is relevant to a multiplicity of tasks facing Muslim intellectuals everywhere in the Arab and Islamic world. In the present era, questions of the compatibility of Western models of democracy with Islamic concepts of government have been raised, especially in reference to discussions in the West of civil society in the Middle East. Usually this means some form of multiparty democracy and a more or less favorable record on human rights of a country's citizens. Meanwhile Islamist discourse has stressed the Islamic principle of *shūra* (consultation with the Islamic leader, *amir*) as the chief institutional means of achieving democratic ends in an Islamic state (Turābī in Lowrie 1994). Al-'Ashmawy defines democracy in a universal and not strictly Islamic sense as the right of the people to challenge the government. In its purest sense, democracy is the absolute sovereignty of the people and their natural right to legislate themselves. This notion of a natural right to self-government is derived from the Enlightenment and the French Revolution, unquestionably. However, that an idea may have taken modern shape in a European nation is not an issue for al-'Ashmawy. Democracy presupposes enlightenment, which is itself rooted in widespread literacy and public education. Eastern political and social traditions, he says, are not democratic but historically have been based in autocratic, hierarchical forms of sociopolitical organization based on the absolute right of kings and princes (*mūlūk*) to rule. Obedience to institutions and figures of authority has been stressed more than has the right of the common people to rule.

Further elaboration of this point requires a more extensive consideration of shūra, which, as al-ʿAshmawy describes it, has been hailed as Islam's answer to Western democracy. This shūra, he says, is "only the sheikhs [religious scholars] talking to one another" (personal interview, January 7, 1995). Dr. Hasan al-Turābī, leader of Sudan's Islamist National Islamic Front and a founder and leader of Sudan's Muslim Brothers in the 1960s, claims that "all modern Islamic movements are highly democratic. . . . They are based on *majlīs shūra*, which is 100 percent elected, and the leader is elected, and he is accountable, and so their model is democratic" (quoted in Lowrie 1994, 9). Islamic movements are essentially grassroots, populist movements, which, if scrutinized, are highly democratic, Turābī claims. On the other hand, shūra, al-ʿAshmawy points out, can turn the strong religious leaders, the *ʿulamā*', into a powerful majority, which allows them—with the power of religion and the state—to be the only ones who exercise the rights of full citizenship. Also, non-Muslim minorities become persons with less than full citizenship. This is antidemocratic, wrong, and inappropriate to the modern era. Power sharing between a Muslim majority and non-Muslim minorities will not work so long as the religious right is the majority or represents the majority interests.

The matter of the rights of non-Muslims in an Islamic state has been taken up by modern Muslim reformers, such as Mahmoud Muhammad Taha, Sudanese founder of the Republican Brothers, an Islamic reformist group, who was himself executed for the crime of apostasy during the last months of the Islamist phase of the Numieri regime in 1985. The Republican Brothers seek reform of contemporary Islamic society precisely on the point of the inability of traditional Islamic institutions to permit proportional democratic representation to non-Muslims and to women. Taha's *Second Message of Islam* does not refer to any new revelations but to a reinterpretation of the holy sources appropriate to the contemporary period. Such interpretation includes acknowledgment of a Qur'ānic base for establishing the equality of rights and status for women and non-Muslim minorities in the modern Islamic state or a state governed by a Muslim majority. This, al-'Ashmawy claims, is not possible under most current states where powerful Muslim interests predominate. Al-'Ashmawy's writings helped to halt the political move in the early 1980s toward the codification of *Sharī'a* (Islamic law) as the only state law in force in Egypt. Similarly, a move was blocked to frame an Islamic constitution in Egypt, which al-'Ashmawy and other humanist intellectuals feared would discriminate against Egypt's Coptic Christian minority.

Mahmoud Taha's struggle against Islamization in the Sudan failed, and his fate was sealed, according to Abdullai An-Na'im, Taha's disciple and translator of his works, once the Republican Brothers opposed the 1983 imposition of Sharī'a as state law (Taha 1987, 10–13). This move occurred despite Sudan's nearly one-third non-Muslim minority population and an activist women's movement that had liberalized the application of the Sharī'a in the Sudan (see Fluehr-Lobban 1987). Taha's fate was inevitable, according to al-'Ashmawy's assessment of contemporary governments with pronounced Islamist tendencies. Cases of alleged apostasy from Islam like those of Taha in Sudan and Professor Abu Zeid more recently in Egypt represent the open face of public ideological struggle being waged by the Islamists against reformist tendencies in contemporary Islamic societies.

Perhaps the most profound moral expression of humanism within Islam is to be found in the growing human rights movement in the Middle East and the Islamic world. Because the international human rights movement is historically associated with Western intellectual traditions, from the Enlightenment to the United Nations Universal Declaration of Human Rights, it can be easily dismissed by the Islamists, who claim that the concept of human rights is a foreign, Western one imposed on Muslim peoples. All of the necessary human rights can be found within Islam. Al-ʿAshmawy would agree; however he would argue that interpretations by human beings—especially the state-controlled ʿulamāʾ—as well as the evidence of historical experience show that human rights have not always been fully observed by governments, Islamic and secular alike.

Those who promote the cause of human rights, like Muhammad Saʿid al-ʿAshmawy, have been accused of following or imitating the West. The debate about human rights in the Middle East has been summarized and reviewed as a complex dialogue about human relations within nations, dealing with the rights of women and minorities, and in the international arena, where local governments can face political and economic sanctions over alleged human rights violations (Dwyer 1991). Claiming that such ideas are foreign or Western and, therefore, "un-Islamic" or "anti-Islamic" can be a convenient excuse to be exempted from international human rights standards. Human rights activists in Middle East countries often are not only challenging the state but are accused of anti-Islamic activity as well. As a jurist, Muhammad Saʿid al-ʿAshmawy has been recognized by the Lawyers' Committee for Human Rights (October 18, 1994, New York City) "for his work to protect human rights and promote the rule of law." The plaque he was given contains the quotation from the Universal Declaration that "all human beings are born free and equal in dignity and human rights."

Al-ʿAshmawy sees two clear attitudes toward human rights in the Islamic world today. One is the extremist Islamic militant view, seeing rights from within Islam as primary and more fundamental than human rights. This view sees God's law, the Sharīʿa, as meeting all human needs to legislate themselves. Human rights advocacy is, therefore, superfluous. Al-ʿAshmawy would probably agree, provided that states governed by Muslims in the name of Islam recognized and observed the human rights of all citizens.

The alternative view has been characterized as the liberal, enlightened view, based on the argument that not all of the legal rules mentioned in the Qurʾān are permanent, that some are temporary. Al-ʿAshmawy notes that slavery and slave harems were mentioned in the Qurʾān and were not abrogated, yet they have fallen by the wayside and are now forbidden by law. In other words, society changed and human interpretation and application altered with changing conditions. Under the liberal view, women and men have equal rights; all humans are entitled to the right of free choice of religion, without fear of coercion, and all humans have the right of free speech. Without equivocation, al-ʿAshmawy sees one ethical and moral code for all human beings in all places. No one should be excluded on any ground, and any discrimination is fundamentally unethical. States do not give rights; the state can only acknowledge the basic humanity in all and the human rights that derive from this fact. As he writes in this book, in the liberal movement "justice precedes punishment, the spirit is more important than the text, and humanity is one community."

Islam and the State: Islamist and Liberal Humanist Perspectives Contrasted

Virtually all of the Islamic revivalists agree on a common goal of creating an Islamic state, but they do not agree on what the nature of that state should be. The contemporary dialogue between East and West on the subject of the Islamic state focuses upon the compatibility of such states with democracy, meaning democratic traditions as they have been developed in the West. Usually this is interpreted as evidenced by elections with leaders and representatives elected within a context of multiple parties competing for political office.

"Islamic government is not democratic as in the West," writes Islamist thinker Ahmad Shālaby. "In the first place much of what is called democracy is not democratic at all, although all states, east and west, pretend to be democratic. The difference is that Islam offers many laws that cannot be neglected or changed, and are not subject to consultation or discussion, such as the law of inheritance, marriage and divorce." Democracy gives the people the opportunity to design their own laws (Shālaby 1970, 395–96), which is not an option for much of God's law in the Sharī'a.

It is said that the ruler is the shade of God on earth and that sixty years of an unjust Imam are preferable to one night without an Imam (ibid., 381). Consultation (shūra) is essential on the widest scale possible, including the use of plebiscite. Islamic government receives its authority from the people and not from God, Shālaby writes, and as the people have received this authority from God they have the right to withdraw it. Islamic government is not theocratic because it exists by the will of the people. No caliph has the kind of power of infallibility that the pope has; caliphs serve only to execute the religious creeds. The caliph, Shālaby argues, is a common Muslim whose only role is to implement the religious creed.

There is no disagreement among al-'Ashmawy reformers, like Muhammad Abduh, and the Islamists that Islamic government derives its authority from the Umma, the world community of Muslims, but they disagree about the role of the caliph as the leader of a theocratic entity. In a proper Islamic state the ruler exists for the welfare of humanity, not the reverse, as has been the case historically. The jurist Muhammad Abduh argued against the Western criticism of Islamic unity of religion and the state, saying the West lives by a double standard on this. The queen of England refers to herself as the queen of the Protestants while the U.S. government engages in extensive use of Christian symbols.

Other Islamist thinkers, like Dr. Hasan al-Turābī, agree that the Islamic state derives its authority from the Umma. Moreover, according to Turābī (in Esposito 1983, 243), the Islamic state is not a sovereign entity but is subject to the higher norms of the Sharī'a that represent the will of God. The ruler's powers should not be absolute. The Islamic state is not primordial but is subject to the Umma, and the jurists purposefully eliminated the state as a source of law in their *usūl al-fiqh* (the sources of religious law). The legislative arm of government was assumed by the jurists themselves. It is only under secularized governments that Muslims have felt the bitter oppression of totalitarianism. The good in secular government can be incorporated so long as it is not contrary to the Sharīʿa. Insurgent Islam is seeking to make up for the historic failure to realize Islam fully. European colonialism contained or suppressed Islamic institutions, and now the moment has arrived for the actualization of the Islamic potential.

Contrary to the Islamist view outlined here, al-ʿAshmawy argues that when Islam became wedded to politics and empire, its course was radically altered by political manipulation. Thus al-ʿAshmawy opposes any form of Islamic government as untrustworthy and potentially corruptible by its claim to religious legitimacy. Islam, if properly understood and applied in a just society, is in no need of reform and is adequate in its pristine form. However, there is no just society today, Islamic or otherwise, and the days of a pristine Islam faded dramatically after the first four of the rightly guided caliphs.

Al-ʿAshmawy is likewise critical of "democratic" elections, Egyptian-style, with 99 percent approval of a candidate or referendum. Democracy is far more than elections, he says; indeed such "elections" have been showcased in a variety of autocratic, dictatorial countries that have been obvious shams of democracy. Often the enlightened citizens, the intellectuals, boycott these elections because of their false pretenses and propagandist intent.

The principle of separating politics from religion is critical, al-ʿAshmawy argues. Politics must be practiced unfettered by religion. Moreover, the proper relationship between the individual and the state is one of citizenship, not religion. Were the state recast by an Islamic constitution, which al-ʿAshmawy vehemently opposed when President Anwar Sadat took under consideration such a proposal in the late 1970s, it would mean the denigration of the status of non-Muslims to second-class citizens. Beyond the moral and humanist issues, al-ʿAshmawy has strongly criticized the Egyptian government's treatment of the Coptic Christian minority because of his overriding fear of a theocratic state. Since 1977 Egypt has prohibited the formation of any political party on religious grounds; this move was originally intended to block decades-old attempts by the Muslim Brotherhood to form a political party. However, al-ʿAshmawy does argue for the continuation of the formal relationship between the state and Islamic religious institutions, such as Al-Azhar Mosque–University and the government-appointed Muftī (the highest religious authority in Egypt), without which he fears the potential for a religious front to develop against civil society.

A vital part of both Islamist and reformist views of the modern state lies with their mutual criticism of the ʿulamāʾ, who are frequently state-appointed officials who have been accused of falling prey to opportunism and collaborationism. Since the ʿulamāʾ symbolize the official state position on religious matters, they are the obvious targets of opponents of the state. Their *fatwas* (religious interpretations having the weight of law) are often regarded more as reflections of state domestic and foreign policy than as religiously inspired guidance.

One of the first of the modern Muslim nationalists and early Islamists, Jamal al-Dīn al-Afghānī, reserved his most severe criticism not for the imperialist occupiers of Muslim nations but for the backward ʿulamāʾ: "Since the state of our ʿulamāʾ has been demonstrated, we can only say that our ʿulamāʾ at this time are like a very narrow wick on top of which is a very small flame that neither lights its surroundings nor gives light to others. What kind of scholar is it who does not enlighten even his own home? Our ʿulamāʾ have divided science into two parts, one is Muslim Science (Sharīʿa, *usūl al-dīn*) and the other European science, and they forbid the teaching of the useful sciences; science is a noble thing with no connection to a nation or religion—our ʿulamāʾ delight in the study of Aristotle, but regard Galileo, Newton and Kepler as infidels—there is no incompatibility between science, knowledge and the Islamic faith" (al-Afghānī, in Donahue and Esposito 1982, 19).

The fact is that the core of Islam manifested through the Sharīʿa as interpreted by the ʿulamāʾ over the centuries has taken the form of a rigid and prescriptive system that is not characteristic of earlier Islamic thought in its formative period. The challenge of today's world and its changing conditions requires flexibility, not rigidity; the latter only deepens the current crisis in Islamic societies (Hanafi 1970).

Context of al-'Ashmawy's Work: Extremist Militants in Egypt

Muhammad Sa'id al-'Ashmawy began to write on legal, social, and theological subjects once the Islamic militants in Egypt began their activism toward the implementation of an Islamist agenda, especially after the assassination of Sadat in the early 1980s. Sheikh 'Omer 'Abdel Rahman captured the international headlines as a "fundamentalist" and "fanatic" in the early 1990s, but Egyptian intellectuals who are challenging Islamic extremists from within an Islamic framework and methodology are not given an equal hearing on the world's stage of ideas. Al-'Ashmawy's critical analysis of the contemporary Islamist movement in Egypt can be generalized to comparable movements throughout the Islamic world. The same extremism that killed Sadat is more extensive today and the *Jamā'at al-Islāmīya* (Islamic militant groups) have only grown, despite more intensive and focused Egyptian government repression. In his day Sadat was certainly not a popular politician among the Egyptian people, and he was widely referred to as "Shah No. 2," after the Iranian revolution, or as a modern-day pharaoh. He was accused of living a lifestyle comparable to that of the shah of Iran, and few outside the West mourned his passing. The local focus on the unpopularity of Sadat may have masked the greater truth of his assassination, which was a profound political shift away from secular nationalism toward the Islamist agenda. From that time on, Egyptian political discourse has been dominated by ideological response and multiple political reactions to the Islamic extremists.

Muhammad Sa'id al-'Ashmawy courageously entered this field and became one of the most prominent voices against the extremists. His importance lies in the fact that his frame of reference is not Western and therefore not easily dismissed by Muslims at home and abroad; his critical analysis is grounded in Islamic theology and methodology.

A turning point may have been reached with the assault by Islamists on Naguib Mahfouz, Egyptian Nobel Laureate. During his recovery, al-ʿAshmawy visited him several times. Mahfouz has been another courageous intellectual who took a critical stand against Islamic extremism. He entered the dialogue in 1977 on the issue of the application of the Sharīʿa as comprehensive law in the state of Egypt. He argued that in most ways Egyptian society is not operating as an Islamic society; if it begins to apply the Sharīʿa punishments (*ḥūdūd*), it is protecting a non-Islamic government by Islamic punishments. In reality, Egyptians make and sell wine, set up gambling casinos and nightclubs in tourist centers, and engage in many non-Islamic or anti-Islamic practices. The twin essential vices, Mahfouz argues, are debilitating poverty and excessive wealth: "I fear dire consequences if we resort to Islamic ḥūdūd to protect conditions unworthy of Islamic protection. Every Muslim would dream of an all encompassing Sharīʿa law, but we are a schizophrenic society; half of the Muslim believes, prays, fasts, and makes the pilgrimage, while the other half neutralizes these values by the use of banks, courts, in the streets, the cinemas, and at home in front of the TV" (in Donahue and Esposito 1982, 240).

It is easy to close bars and mandate a new dress code for women, but, asks Mahfouz, what about more far-reaching banking and current economic practices? asks Mahfouz. It is no longer possible to give sole allegiance to God and kingdom as in the old days of the caliphates; that is history. Indeed, the Arabs fought against the abode of the Caliph in World War I by siding with the British colonial power against the Ottoman Empire. The modern contradictions are indeed challenging, but God has given us the gift of intellect to provide a way for interpretation and application of Islamic principles to the reality of present-day life. Statements like these were probably the kind of sentiments that provoked the attack on one of the twentieth-century's great literary figures.

Al-ʿAshmawy critiques the militant doctrine in Islam in what amounts to a fundamental response to their ideas from the humanistic core of

Islam. First, he points out that the militants see Islam as the sole, valid, and complete faith, making all non-Muslims infidels. This position, which abrogates the previous prophetic traditions, places the great faiths in conflict with one another rather than as equals that can be collaborators. The result is that the two zones, Dār al-Islām and Dār al-Harb, the abode of Muslims and the abode of war, will be in permanent confrontation until non-Muslims are converted to Islam. Second, by stressing that politics is a necessary part of Islam, the militants have in effect elevated the political domain to one of the pillars of the faith. Politics is certainly a part of Islamic history, but it is neither a pillar of the faith nor a cornerstone of dogma, while a religious state and a religious party within a state are unacceptable. The militant doctrine conceives of the ruler in an Islamic state as acting under divine command, a dangerous idea, he warns. The Sharīʿa, which militants seek to impose as state law, mainly comprises historical jurisprudence, which is a reflection of Islamic political history. The legal rules derived from the Qurʾān are relatively few in number, perhaps only eighty of the Qurʾān's 6,236 verses, and are mainly in the area of personal status matters. In short, he argues that the case for the implementation of the Sharīʿa as the basis for an Islamic state has been overstated. In the end, al-ʿAshmawy argues, the militant doctrine in Islam not only poses a danger and a threat to humanity and peace but also undermines Islam itself, falsifying its great teachings and distorting its humanistic attitudes.

Al-ʿAshmawy's Thought in the Tradition of Islamic Reform

Muhammad Abduh evoked the spirit of reform as Egypt's Grand Muftī. In his own time he was a controversial figure, especially to those who thought his compromises with the West went too far. His activism led to periods of exile from Egypt, in Paris with al-Afghānī and later in Beirut. Abduh ultimately served the Egyptian government well; his reintroduction of the idea of issuing fatwas to private individuals on matters of law and conscience formed the basis of many reforms that accommodated

British rule and its desire to modernize Islamic institutions. However, taking Abduh's reforms as a whole, al-ʿAshmawy detects no underlying foundation or methodology for his fatwas, which, as a result, may appear separated, idiosyncratic, and unconnected to any more general formulation or philosophy.

Muhammad Abduh was a strong advocate of the role of reason, and he defended the right of humans to interpret and change the laws of Islam, the Sharīʿa, rather than adhering to blind attachment to traditional opinions (Donahue and Esposito 1982, 24). Islamic jurisprudence (al-fiqh), after all, is made up of a corpus of human interpretation of the holy sources of the religion—Qurʾān and Sunna. Al-ʿAshmawy develops this further today, saying that humans have the right, indeed the obligation, to change the laws as societal conditions change. Many conservative Muslim thinkers would argue that only God makes laws or is capable of changing them; it is the role of humans only to listen to God, using reason to interpret His will.

Muhammad Saʿid al-ʿAshmawy offers new paths of interpretation and thought. Al-ʿAshmawy's ideas are more revolutionary than reformist as they deal with the foundation of ideas in Islam and in all of the faiths. The totality of al-ʿAshmawy's thinking offers new directions for interpretation and renewal of Islam. By providing a new methodology for understanding the holy sources of Qurʾan and Sunna, he offers solutions to the traditional problems of Islamic interpretation. In doing so, he believes that he is freeing the Muslim mind by helping to turn it toward more systematic, more objective, and ultimately more scientific thinking.

The essential framework for understanding al-ʿAshmawy's ideas and approach toward a new Islamic interpretation can be summarized in three parts. First, he offers precise definitions of basic terms, such as "Sharīʿa," which he sees as having been historically misinterpreted and misapplied. Sharīʿa is defined as Islamic law as it has been interpreted by the religious scholars; Sharīʿa is mainly man-made and not divine, as is often alleged. According to al-ʿAshmawy, the greater part of what is considered Sharīʿa is not what has been revealed in the Qurʾān, but what the scholars have determined are legal rules based on their interpretations of Qurʾānic texts. The original meaning of Sharīʿa, as path, method, or way, was lost after the first generation of Muslims, and over time it came to mean the legal rules themselves rather than "the way" to conduct a good Muslim life. Today Sharīʿa refers to Islamic jurisprudence.

Demonstrating the essential differences between Sharīʿa and fiqh was an early and central part of al-ʿAshmawy's thinking, a theoretical distinction made all the more clear from his practice and career as a jurist. Since most of what is considered Sharīʿa is actually fiqh, a man-made science of jurisprudence, not divinely revealed, it follows that it has an historical development that can and does change. I recall a somewhat awkward discussion with professors and sheikhs at Al-Azhar Islamic University in 1983 in which I erred by referring in Arabic to the "evolution" (*tatwir*) of the Sharīʿa; the Sharīʿa, in their view, does not evolve or change. The development of fiqh within various historical contexts where ʿulamāʾ have put forth their opinions should be a clear process in al-ʿAshmawy's view, but over time these interepretations have come to be viewed as fixed, as divinely inspired, and have reified what is in fact a man-made system of law.

Second, al-ʿAshmawy's thinking provides a methodology of interpretation for whatever subject by working at the level of the fundamentals of the faith. The basic method is one of viewing the interpretation of the Holy Qurʾān in historical context, considering that the revealed texts covered a span of twenty-two years. By using the historical method of interpretation al-ʿAshmawy believes that Muslims should find the reasons for the revelations and in doing so can avoid the contradictory interpretations found in Muslim thinking. By applying the historical method he believes that the problem of apparently contradictory texts is resolved; in fact, most of the problems of Islamic interpretation are also resolved. For example, he takes the disturbing issue of jihād, which can lead to ideas of war and intolerance of non-Muslims as dwellers in the Dār al-

Ḥārb, the abode of war, or as kāfirun, unbelievers. Using the historical method it can be shown that jihād is based upon Qur'ānic verses that were temporary. In proper historical context jihād can be justified for a time, but after the establishment of Islam, its growth, spread, and institutionalization in diverse societies, jihād can no longer be justified. According to al-ʿAshmawy, the Islamist militants are wrong for spreading the idea of jihād, thereby separating the Muslims and non-Muslims and threatening relations between people of different faiths.

Likewise, the institution of slavery is mentioned in Qur'ānic texts with multiple references to the treatment of slaves along with the positive religious benefit of manumission. While slavery is mentioned in many of the revealed texts, it was never canceled or abolished in any subsequent text. Nonetheless slavery has generally disappeared as a human system and has been legally removed from many Muslim societies. This also shows that certain verses were revealed to be temporary and not permanent. Many of the verses cited by the militants, especially regarding jihād and the treatment of non-Muslims, were wrongly interpreted as fixed and ahistorical rather than having a specific historic context that no longer exists.

Third, al-ʿAshmawy provides a structure that is systematic allowing the process of constructing a new Islamic thought to unfold. This is a new feature for the Muslim mind, he believes, which is more accustomed to repetition and recitation without the application of critical thought. The critical facility and the construction of a systematic analysis by which Qur'ānic verses might be interpreted on a structural level has not been undertaken. Al-ʿAshmawy points to the more than 6,000 verses in 114 chapters of the Qur'ān with only 80 verses pertaining to Sharīʿa. This is a point of construction in the Qur'ān, the analysis of which leads to discoveries of deeper structure in the Holy Book revealing religious intent beyond the literal interpretations of verses that the Islamic world has so far provided.

William Shepard, in his 1996 article assessing the writing of al-ʿAshmawy and the application of the Sharīʿa in Egypt, sees him as a secular reformer in the tradition of ʿAli ʿAbd al-Rāziq and Muhammad Khala-fallah. However, al-ʿAshmawy expands upon that tradition of reform in Egypt with a contemporary call for nothing short of a reformation in Islamic law. With respect to gender and other human rights issues, he argues that an important arena of human rights is women's rights. He points out that Islamic traditions interpreted by male ʿulamāʾ have failed to achieve equal rights for women. There has been confusion between Arab social customs and Islam as a faith. He argues that Islamic faith is a dynamic force with the ability to follow the path of progress only if women are recognized as having full and equal rights.

Al-ʿAshmawy finds problematical the use of the term *fundamentalism* to describe religious extremism in Islam. He calls himself a fundamental-ist in the sense that he and every Muslim scholar or practitioner accept and respect the fundamentals of the faith, the Five Pillars, Qurʾān and Sunna. He distinguishes his own "rational fundamentalism," based on the fundamentals set by the Qurʾān, from "political fundamentalism," which extracts some verses from their Qurʾānic context and separates them from the causes of revelation (Shepard 1996, 44).

The use of reason by al-ʿAshmawy underlies the need for reform in Islam, while the central place for human reason has always been a key element in the world's humanist traditions. The Qurʾān is a book that exalts respect for reason, the shaping of the individual through research, knowledge, and the use of reason and reflection. For the Muslims it is the most perfect of the religious books because it is not meant for a single time or place but for all humanity for all time. This core, essentially hu-manist vision of al-ʿAshmawy takes this a step further with the hope that the elaboration of humanist values within the Islamic Umma will bring about a reformation in Islam in the twenty-first century.

An Islamic Reformation?

Islamic revival needs to be distinguished from Islamic reformation. Re-vivalism has been a consistent feature of Islamic history, inherent in the logic and experience of Muslims in history (Voll 1986, 169). Revivalists have appeared periodically as a regular occurrence, nineteenth-century examples being the Wahabist movement in Arabia and the Mahdist movement in the Sudan. It is clear that the current Muslim revival is affected by the interaction between Muslim and Western cultures. But what al-ʿAshmawy and those who would agree with him are addressing is something more fundamental than religio-political revival; it is a basic reformulation of Islamic institutions and thought as a response to deep crises in Muslim societies.

Contrary to the dire predictions that abound in the West of a funda- mentalist "return to the dark ages" in the Islamic world, in fact intellec- tual ferment and struggle have never been greater or more lively than during the current period in the Islamic Middle East, with major ramify- ing effects in the Muslim world in general. One of the countries central to this lively intellectual tradition has always been Egypt. Not only have many of the important Islamic reformers been Egyptian, but some of the most conservative "fundamentalist" figures, such as the founder of the Muslim Brotherhood, Hasan al-Banna, also has his roots in Egyptian soil.

Many of the revivalists, the so-called fundamentalists, are classically trained legal scholars, jurists, and clerics, perhaps with limited interest in or exposure to the world of ideas beyond Islam. Some may be familiar only with their own language and that of the Qurʾān. Ayatollah Kho- meini readily comes to mind; his years of exile in France were largely spent in isolation. Others who are familiar with Western languages and cultures may have studied in the West and can readily utilize that knowl- edge to be critical of the West. Dr. Hasan al-Turābī of Sudan, besides being a major historical figure among the Muslim Brothers, holds ad- vanced degrees from English and French universities. What unites lib- erals like al-ʿAshmawy and more conservative Islamist thinkers of the nineteenth and twentieth centuries is their common belief in the continu- ing relevance of Islam and its ability to provide a sufficient framework for life in the twentieth century and beyond.

Those contemporary Muslim thinkers who challenge a passive role for humans, who openly criticize Islamic fatalism and who see human beings as agents of their own destiny, are often cast as reformers or non-religious secularists. But they may in fact be part of a more fundamental process—that is, an Islamic reformation. In this work al-'Ashmawy openly and directly addresses the need for Islamic reformation, which he characterizes as a renewal of the Islamic mind, its ethical code, and respect for human rights, including women's emancipation. Without such a reformation, Muslims will be excluded from the international community and will be unable to play their just and proper role in human history.

The West's monochromic view of Islam is beginning to be replaced with the first glimmerings of a more complex view of Islamic movements in questions like "which Islam?" and "whose Islam?" Why is Islamic government being called for in states where Islamic government is already in practice—for example, in Saudi Arabia? This interesting phenomenon suggests that the struggle for change is much deeper than a matter of individual state politics. It is a part of a more fundamental rebellion against a social order that is corrupt, decadent, and impious. The collaboration of the 'ulamā' with essentially non-Islamic governments, and their collaboration with the ruling families and elites, ends with the ultimate dependence of all on non-Islamic and imperialistic powers (Rahnema 1994, 5). Add to this the rampant failures of Arab nationalism as a prevailing secular model of state and society in the Middle East and Muslim world, and the search for alternatives in religion that are compatible with modern life is reasonable, if not inevitable. This overarching reality in many contemporary Islamic societies leads to cynicism, alienation, and finally to the construction of new models of religion and society.

Bassam Tibi (1990), in arguing for the necessity of an Islamic reformation, notes that the secularization of Christianity did not bring about its demise. Western industrial culture remains essentially Christian in character despite having been secularized. Allowing commercial and business transactions on Sundays has not threatened the existence of churches. However, some politically active Muslims, perhaps anxious to defend their religion, tend to equate secularism with atheism. Overcoming underdevelopment, Tibi argues, means joining the secular economy and industrial society. The backward-looking revival of the sacred—that is, Islamic "fundamentalism"—while it may be important for the psychological well-being of the social group, is not a mechanism for overcoming economic underdevelopment.

Tibi continues that the Muslim societies are economically underdeveloped, which is the result of the close correspondence between the sacred and the political. The backward-looking cultural restoration of Islam (as in Iran) offers no real or permanent solution. This is an aggressive defensive-cultural response (Tibi 1990, 196). Politics therefore must be desacralized in Islamic society; he advocates a secularism that is not a profanity but that will protect religion from exploitation for political purposes. Muhammad Sa'id al-'Ashmawy makes precisely the same point, that religion must be protected from state exploitation in the modern era, unlike the blending of religion and the state in the traditional model of Islamic government.

Al-'Ashmawy believes that a reformation of Islamic institutions is essential as the future of Islam unfolds within state and global societies in the coming century. Moreover, widespread corruption in such key governments as Egypt's will only fuel the conservative and antireformist Islamic movement. The sheikhs at Al-Azhar University are often so preoccupied with opposing the Egyptian government that they may issue interpretations (fatwas) solely on that basis. When the Egyptian government was embarrassed at the Cairo United Nations Population Conference by revelations that female circumcision is still widely practiced in Egypt, the sheikhs at Al-Azhar defended the "religious" basis of the practice mainly from a desire to oppose the government, according to al-'Ashmawy (personal interview, January 1995). Female circumcision, or female genital mutilation, is a pre-Islamic practice common in northeastern Africa and the Sahel but not required by Islam or any other faith, and it is a distinct sociocultural tradition. Contradictions like this will continue to mount, al-'Ashmawy believes, until the forces of reform overwhelm the old order.

An Islamic reformation means renunciation of the doctrine of absolute superiority of Islam and Muslims. This would reflect a humanistic vision of the multireligious modern world. Al-'Ashmawy, a devout Muslim, nonetheless demonstrates a deep respect for faith and practice outside Islam. Islamists, on the other hand, adhere to an exclusivist view of their religion as the final revelation, complete and without equal. Hasan al-Banna, the prototypical Islamist activist and founder of the Muslim Brotherhood in Egypt in 1928, wrote in *The New Renaissance* that the decisive factor in the triumph of Islamization of government and society is the perfection of Islam. The excellence of the Islamic principles of collective organization over everything known to humans until now is demonstrable, and for the good of humankind in general Muslims must move toward a return to their religion (in Donahue and Esposito 1982, 83–84).

By contrast, al-'Ashmawy's humanist vision sees the connections among the Abrahamic faiths and their critical need for coexistence in the modern era.

Islamic "Fundamentalism," Islamic Humanism, and Relations with the West

Al-'Ashmawy, like other writers today, does not use the term *fundamentalism* to describe what he thinks is better understood as extremism. The fundamentals of Islam (usūl al-dīn)—the Qur'ān and Sunna and the practice of the Five Pillars—are not in dispute. No one, liberal or conservative, is questioning the fundamentals of the faith; matters of interpretation of the sources and application of these ideas in contemporary society are what are at issue.

Unquestionably, the struggle for Islamic identity and direction has taken place in the modern period in the context of the dynamic that has shaped the encounter between East and West. This has included imbalances and hierarchical relations such as those characterizing colonialism, the postcolonial economic dependency of the East, and, perhaps most important, the creation of the state of Israel as a Western entity with a history perceived in the East as reflecting anti-Arab and anti-Muslim attitudes in the West. In the face of political conquest and hence the threat of linguistic and cultural loss or assimilation, the religion of Islam and its institutions provides the one powerful, indigenous framework to challenge and counter the Western onslaught. The 'ulamā', who sought to protect Islamic institutions during the heyday of the European colonial imprint upon Muslim societies, deserve praise and recognition for the role they played in religious and cultural survival in the face of Western imperial designs and administration. Indeed, the dynamic between East and West has rarely been balanced and bilateral, especially during the last two centuries of colonial imposition of Western culture and the selective suppression of aspects of Arab-Muslim culture. Secular nationalist movements provided one form of response to colonialism that were successful in the transition to political independence. Islamically inspired responses, in the end, were not crucial to the success of the drive for independence, although they were part of broad anticolonial resistance. As postindependence secular nationalist governments have repeatedly failed to deliver on promises of economic security and political equality, Islamist challenges have grown and spread throughout the Middle East and in the Arab-Muslim world. The better known cases, such as the movement epitomized by Ayatollah Khomeini of Iran, mask the diversity and complexity of the discussion now taking place throughout the Muslim world.

For Muhammad Abduh the issue at the end of the nineteenth century was whether Islam could be relevant for the modern world, not whether one could both be a Muslim and live in the modern world. This was the period when European imperialism was exerting its maximum political and cultural influence. When Muslims return to their religion and call for its reform, this is not insurrection against Europe, he insisted. He thought that Muslims could profitably learn from Europe but that they should not engage in indiscriminate borrowing or blind imitation of the West; those who did so became the enemy from within.

Other acknowledged Muslim "modernists," such as the Algerian phi-
losopher Muhammad Arkoun, turned to the study of Western thought,
including Marxism initially, only to return to Islamic philosophy as a
living, vital source. He wrote both on traditional Islamic philosophy and
on the confrontation of Islamic thought with modernism (Nasr 1987,
192). His recently translated *Rethinking Islam: Common Questions, Uncommon Answers* (1994; titled *Ouvertures sur l'Islam* in the original French) is
a call to Muslims not to fear the use of reason in thinking about Islam in
the contemporary era, and it is a challenge to Westerners to reflect upon
their biases, held largely in ignorance of the Islamic faith.

Taha Husayn (1889–1973), another of Egypt's great writers, points
out that Egypt was one of the first of the Islamic states to recover her
ancient, forgotten personality without apparent contradiction. "There is
a struggle between the old and new, as evidenced in the Shari'a and
Egyptian law, a mix of the two. The fact is that day by day we become
more western and draw closer to Europe, yet no one is advocating a
return to rule of law and government of Pharaonic, Greco-Roman, or
early Islamic times. In another era it was the Europeans who were borrowing from the Islamic world during the Middle Ages. They did just
then what we are doing now. Obviously then I am pleading for a selective
approach to European culture, not wholesale and indiscriminate borrowing" (quoted in Donahue and Esposito 1982, 77).

In marked contrast, Hasan al-Banna (1906–1949) formulated the Muslim Brotherhood ideology specifically in reaction to the Western presence
in Egypt and the Islamic world. In the *The New Renaissance* he wrote that
the final Islamization of society and nation would come because of the
failure of the West in following the materialist path alone, one of sin,
passion, drink, and women, and that the decisive factor in overcoming
the Western onslaught was the perfection of Islam.

Al-'Ashmawy acknowledges no such confrontation between so-called
modernism and Islam; indeed, he fears that the present reactionary Islamist movements place the Islamic world on a collision course with the
West, headed for a historic confrontation that the Muslim world will

surely lose. His vision comprehends an already existing world system of material conditions that could potentially include the spiritual as well. Without a synthesis of Islamic values with global technology and world civilization, Islamic societies, in al-'Ashmawy's view, will be left in a hopelessly backward position, unable to catch up with world trends in coming centuries.

In this world system al-'Ashmawy maintains extensive contacts outside Egypt, in Europe, North America, in the Arab and Islamic world, and in India. He recognizes the multiple examples of mutual cultural borrowing that have occurred between East and West, North and South. In part, the delayed recognition and acknowledgment of al-'Ashmawy as a significant thinker have to do with the perception (in the West as well as in the Islamic world) that he is an apologist for the West and that his writings represent a defense of the West. Al-'Ashmawy has been critical of both East and West, and he has praised traditions in both cultural-historical regions. He does not see the West as bad or the global culture that it has spawned as necessarily all evil. He does call for selective judgment in receiving and retaining materials and ideas from the West, but he points to the general benefits of the spread of Western-based technology, as in computers, for example.

Contemporary religious revival is partly a continuing response to the dominance of the East by the West, but it has also become an indigenous response in the present era where Arab nationalism has been eclipsed and Islamist politics actively contest for political control. This pan-Islamic resurgence, however, is not of a single type; it has many voices and expressions throughout the Islamic and Arab worlds. Too often we in the West stereotype Islamic activism as associated only with extremism, terrorism, fanaticism, and anti-Western sentiments. Threats and misdeeds of extremists capture the headlines, as evidenced by events surrounding the arrest of Sheikh 'Omer 'Abdel Rahman and the alleged conspirators in the bombing of the World Trade Center in 1993. The negative image of Islam as a religion that promotes violence and terrorism was underscored during the hours immediately after the Oklahoma City bombing in 1995, when the longest shadow of suspicion fell upon Arabs and Muslims until indications more accurately pointed toward domestic terrorism. Few would have imagined the scenario in Israel when Prime Minister Yitzhak Rabin was assassinated in 1995 by a Jewish extremist and not a Palestinian Arab or a Muslim terrorist. Despite mounting evidence to the contrary, the stereotype of Islam and terrorism is still reinforced habitually in journalistic reporting from the Middle East, where the focus on Islamic extremism leaves the impression that it holds the monopoly on terror and extremism. The term *jihād* once again inspires fear in the West, as though resurrected from another era of relations between East and West, reminiscent in the current period of the Crusaders' holy war.

Muhammad Sa'id al-'Ashmawy directly addresses jihād, the most sensitive issue in relations between the West and Islam. This word, which excites strong emotions in the West, especially with use of the term by political Islam with movements such as Islamic Jihād, is also the most sensitive and emotional word in the Islamic vocabulary, according to al-'Ashmawy. It literally means "struggle" or "great effort," usually against adverse conditions. Only a minority of Muslims live up to the moral and spiritual meaning of jihād. Initially it meant keeping to one's faith in difficult times. How the word came to mean holy war is a subject al-'Ashmawy considers historically, concluding that jihād was intended for self-defense and not as a means for imposing Islam on non-Muslims. It is unfortunate that jihād has been misunderstood and that its true, deeper meaning has been lost to incorrect ideas of aggression, hostility, and confrontation between East and West.

The fundamental problem of this era of extremism is that Islam has been incorrectly transformed from a faith for all humanity into a political ideology. It has become a source for nationalism and, ultimately, for divisiveness between peoples, religions, and nations. This is contrary to the universalist spirit of Islam and must be challenged by the humanism that is at the core of the Islamic faith. And, in locating that core within Islam, the deeper, universal spiritual humanism that is part of the Abrahamic faiths, and all faiths, will be revealed.

Much of the growing attention that Muhammad Sa'id al-'Ashmawy's writing is gaining consists of interpretation—what various authors understand him to be saying. Some attempt to characterize him as a modernist, secularist, radical Islamist, liberal, or materialist (see Shepard, Murphy), while others (myself and McLean) see him as a universalist thinker and humanist. This volume offers the opportunity to read al-'Ashmawy's own words, and, regardless of categories, it presents the work of a unique and original Muslim thinker for our times.

References Cited

Al-ʿAshmawy, Muhammad Saʿid. 1979. *Usūl al-Shariʿa* (Roots of Islamic law). Cairo: Dar al-Kitab Al-Misri; Beirut: Dar al-Kitab Al-Libnany.

———. 1987. *Al Islam al-Siyasi* (Islam and the political order). Cairo: Dar Sina.

———. 1994. *Islam and the Political Order.* Cultural Heritage and Contemporary Change Series IIA, vol. 1, *Islam.* Preface by George McLean, series general editor. Washington, D.C.: Council for Research in Values and Philosophy, 1994.

Anderson, J. N. D. 1951. *Islamic Law in Africa.* London: Frank Cass.

Arkoun, Mohammed. 1994. *Rethinking Islam: Common Questions, Uncommon Answers.* Translated and edited by Robert D. Lee. Boulder: Westview Press.

Donahue, John J., and John L. Esposito, eds. 1982. *Islam in Transition: Muslim Perspectives.* New York: Oxford University Press.

Dwyer, Kevin. 1991. *Arab Voices: The Human Rights Debate in the Middle East.* Berkeley: University of California Press.

Esposito, John. 1992. *The Islamic Threat: Myth or Reality?* New York: Oxford University Press.

———, ed. 1983. *Voices of Resurgent Islam.* New York: Oxford University Press.

Fluehr-Lobban, Carolyn. 1987. *Islamic Law and Society in the Sudan.* London: Frank Cass.

———. 1990. "Islamization in Sudan: A Critical Assessment." *Middle East Journal* 44(4):610–33.

———. 1994. *Islamic Society in Practice.* Gainesville: University Press of Florida.

Haddad, Yvonne. 1994. "Muhammad Abduh: Pioneer of Islamic Reform." In *Pioneers of Islamic Revival,* edited by Ali Rahnema. London: Zed Books.

Halliday, Fred. 1996. *Islam and the Myth of Confrontation: Religion and Politics in the Middle East.* London: I. B. Tauris.

Hanafi, M. Jamil. 1970. *Islam and the Transformation of Culture.* New York: Asia Publishing House.

Lowrie, Arthur L., ed. 1994. *A Roundtable with Dr. Hasan Turabi: Islam, Democracy, the State and the West.* WISE Monograph Series (1), World and Islam Studies Enterprise, University of South Florida.

Mahfouz, Naguib. 1977. "Debate on the Application of the Sharīʿa in Egypt." *Al-Ahram,* May 17.

McLean, George. *See* al-ʿAshmawy.

Murphy, Julian. 1996. "Islam and Capitalism: The Failure of Islamic Thought in the Twentieth Century, and Much of the External Commentary on That Thought, to Locate Modern Islam and the Middle East Region within a Comprehensive Materialist and Historical Context." Masters thesis, Oxford University.

Nasr, Seyyed Hossein. 1987. *Traditional Islam in the Modern World.* Kuala Lumpur: Foundation for Traditional Studies.

Nettler, Ronald L. 1996. "A Post-Colonial Encounter of Traditions: Muhammad Sa'id al-'Ashmawi on Islam and Judaism." Cited in Murphy 1996.

Rahnema, Ali, ed. 1994. *Pioneers of Islamic Revival.* London: Zed Books.

Shalaby, Ahmad. 1970. *Islam: Belief, Legislation, Morals.* Cairo: Renaissance Book Shop.

Shepard, William E. 1996. "Muhammad Sa'id Al-'Ashmawi and the Application of the Sharī'a in Egypt." *International Journal of Middle East Studies* 28(1):39–58.

Taha, Mahmoud Mohammed. 1987. *The Second Message of Islam.* Translated by Abdullahi Al-Nai'em. Syracuse: Syracuse University Press.

Tibi, Bassam. 1990. *Islam and the Cultural Accommodation of Social Change.* Translated by Clare Krojzl. Boulder: Westview Press.

Voll, John O. 1986. "Revivalism and Social Transformation in Islamic History." *Muslim World* 76(3–4):168–80.

———. 1996. *Islam, Continuity and Change in the Modern World.* 2d ed. Boulder: Westview Press.

PART I

Islam, Judaism, Christianity

One Religion, One Vision, Many Paths

The Development of Religion

I am yesterday, I know tomorrow;
I have become young, I am Osiris;
I have come to lighten the darkness.

The Egyptian Book of the Dead

Religion was conceived or revealed in ancient Egypt with Osiris (c. 6000 B.C.E.). The whole of the religious and mythological system of the Egyptians, as made known to us by texts of later periods, was in a well-developed state, even in the first dynasty (3200 B.C.E.). The general outline of the Egyptian's religion shows us that they possessed a sound, practical form of monotheism and a belief in immortality, which were already ancient, even in the days when the pyramids were built (2500 B.C.E.).

The Egyptians believed in the existence of one Great God, self-produced, self-existent, almighty and eternal, who created the gods, the heavens and the sun, moon and stars in them, and the earth and everything on it, including man and beast, bird, fish and reptile. They believed He existed in everything which He had created and that He was the support of the universe and the Lord of it all. Of this God they never attempted to make any figure, form, likeness or similitude, for they thought that no man could depict or describe Him and that all His attributes were quite beyond man's comprehension.

They said, "God alone, and there is no other God beside Him." Gods were created by the Great God who was proclaimed to be one. The other gods were only names of the various attributes of the One God. The Egyptians believed in the existence of God Almighty and that His commands were performed by a number of gods or emanations or angels. Gods—in this understanding—refer to the angels or to the heroes. There was in the Hieroglyphic language one word, *neter*, to designate either the God or a god or gods, as in most of the oriental languages (for example *Rabb* in Arabic could allude to the Almighty God, to the owner of the business, or to the father of the family). The Egyptian gods symbolized the Almighty God with one flag, the triad with three flags, the triad of the triad (the *ennead*) with nine flags, and the triad of the triads of the triads with twenty-seven flags, but the pronunciation for any symbol was neter, either for the Almighty God or for a god or for gods.

Thus, the Egyptian religion is monotheistic, which manifested itself externally by a symbolic polytheism. The texts assure us that the Egyptians believed in one infinite and eternal God who was without a rival. From these texts we may select the following:

God is one and alone, and none other existeth with Him. God is one, the one who hath made all things. God is from the beginning, and He hath been from the beginning, He hath existed from old and was when nothing else had being. He existed when nothing else existed. God is the eternal one. He is eternal and infinite and endureth forever and aye. God is hidden and no man knoweth His form. No man hath been able to seek out His likeness. His names are innumerable. God is truth. God is life. He was never begotten. He createth, but was never created. God hath made the universe, and He hath created all that therein is. He is the creator of what is in this world and of what was, of what is, and of what shall be. God hath stretched out the heavens and founded the earth. When He hath spoken, it cometh to pass. God is merciful unto those who reverence Him, and He heareth him that calleth upon Him. God knoweth him that acknowledgeth Him, He rewards him that serveth Him, and He protecteth him that follows Him. God is father and mother, the father of fathers, and the mother of mothers.

The central figure of the ancient Egyptian religion was Osiris, and the fundamentals of his cult were the belief in his divinity, death, resurrection and absolute control of the destinies of the bodies and souls of men. The central point of the Osirian religion was the hope of resurrection in a transformed body and the hope of immortality, which could only be realized through the death and resurrection of Osiris.

Osiris was known to the Egyptians by name, which may be transcribed AS-AR or US-AR. In the late dynastic period the first syllable of the name appears to have been pronounced "aus" or "us"; it was made to have the meaning of the word *ʿusr,* which means strength, might, power. Osiris had many pronunciations, one of which was Osir. The Greeks pronounced it Othris, due to their pronunciation and grammar (to add *is* to the end of words). The Arabs—after the Greeks—pronounced it Idris. Some of the Muslim interpreters say that Idris was a prophet who lived in a community in Egypt. Elsewhere they described his mission just as Plutarch did in his book *Isis and Osiris.*

The story is told that Osiris was born, and a voice was heard to proclaim that the Lord of creation was born. In due course Osiris became king of Egypt and devoted himself to civilizing his subjects and to teaching them the craft of the husbandman. He established a code of laws and bade men worship God. Having made Egypt peaceful and a flourishing civilization, Osiris set out to instruct the nations of the world, until he reached India. Osiris was made to suffer death at the hands of his brother, Set, to beget his son Horus by his wife Isis after his death, and then to rise from the dead in a transformed body and to dwell in heaven as the Lord of righteous souls.

Osiris was said to possess two natures—to be partly divine and partly human. The divine part of him did not die. Only the mortal body, which Osiris assumed when he came from the abode of the God to reign upon earth, suffered death. Egyptians believed that Osiris' human nature enabled him to understand the needs, troubles and grief of people and to listen sympathetically to their prayers and that his divine nature gave him powers to help them in this world and the next. Osiris, the divine Ancestor, became the father of the souls of the Egyptians and the symbol of their hope of resurrection and immortality.

The cult of Osiris included the cult of every other god, but the cult of no other god included that of Osiris. The cult of Osiris is the oldest cult in history, literature and the philosophy of religion. Whether or not Osiris traveled to other countries, perhaps as far as India, to preach and teach all over the ancient world, his cult's main theme was preaching and teaching and became the fundamental base for all religious thought, expression and words that followed. This is especially true in the matter of ethics, the doctrine of the man-god, the doctrine of the resurrection, the doctrine of the Judgment Day and the doctrine of immortality.

Osiris was the Lord of Ma'at, which refers to righteousness, justice, good conduct, and order. Ma'at as a goddess of Truth was the counterpart of Thoth—the messenger of God, the Lord of divine words or Lord of the words of God—who was in certain aspects identified with Osiris. Thoth held the word of Osiris to be true or the word made true.

The code of laws Osiris established for humanity was actually one word, Ma'at, which, as mentioned, refers to righteousness, justice, straightness, and order. In addition, Ma'at was both the cosmic conscience and individual conscience. Ma'at was within everyone, Ma'at is man's conscience and God. It was not viewed as a part of the body nor was it influenced by the body. In fact, Ma'at was a permanent self-guide, trial and judgment continuous in life. It was a reflection of the cosmic conscience and order and the true connection between man and universe.

Religion and good conduct was to live with Ma'at and in Ma'at, to act and speak according to Ma'at. As the individual and universal conscience, Ma'at was always strict, clear and fair, beneficial to man, society and the cosmos.

The belief in the efficacy of worship of Osiris, the human-god, who rose from the dead and established himself in the underworld as judge and king, was indelibly impressed on the minds of the Egyptians at a very early period. The reward that Osiris bestowed after death upon his follower was a life led in a region where corn, wine, oil, and water were abundant and where circumstances permitted one to wear white linen robes and white sandals, and where one was able to perform ablutions at will and to repose whenever it pleased one to do so. The followers of Osiris after death possessed their own estate or homestead, where they lived with wife, wives or husband, parents and family. One's heavenly life was to all intents and purposes nothing but a perfect duplication of one's life upon earth. The place of the deceased in heaven is by the side of God. One thirsts not, nor hungers nor is sad. One will be always given "the tree of life."

Osiris could give life because he was life, he could make men rise from the dead because he was the resurrection. Osiris, then, was himself the right, he was the way or path to the right life and to the happy life after death, he was himself the resurrection and the life.

Since Osiris was the God and the judge of the dead, everyone had to pass successfully a postmortem trial in which Osiris was the judge and Horus, his son, was the advocate and the intercessor for the deceased. The deceased entered the hall of trial accompanied by Horus, where she or he declared her or his purity and innocence. Declarations were not enough; the deceased's heart (his individual Maʾat or conscience) had to be weighed as well. On the one side of the scale is placed the feather, the symbol of Maʾat, and on the other side is placed the heart. If the moral integrity of the person had been proven, he or she was proclaimed true of speech and justified in his or her protestations of innocence, and perhaps therefore would gain immortality in the reign of Osiris. Egyptians realized that Osiris was the only God who could grant life everlasting and who had the power to make men and women born again.

Egyptian priests tried to create a perpetual contest between the two great priesthoods of Egypt, namely that of Rà, the sun god, and Osiris. One of the meanings of Osiris' Egyptian name (AS-AR) is "many eyes." It alludes to the relation between Osiris and the sun, the moon and the stars. Osiris was considered the brother of every star, and the sun and the moon were his eyes. It was said that Osiris was the spirit of Rà, the sun god. Since Osiris was identified as the source of light, the priests, perhaps, resorted to a play upon words when they attempted to find etymology for the name of the sun god. They reversed the last two letters of Osiris' name Asar (AR) to Rà.

Actually Osiris was the God of life, the God of the afterlife, the sun god and the god of growth and fertility. Most important, Osiris was the god of conscience. In the end, the doctrine of Osiris prevailed and the attributes of the sun god were ascribed to him. The souls of Osiris and Rà became one, after each God had embraced the other. Osiris absorbed all the concepts, qualities and gods. He was himself Rà and also Thoth. It is mentioned that Osiris is Rà when he speaketh and Thoth when he writeth.

In sum, the religion that originated in ancient Egypt was simply: to have faith in the God and to be straight in conduct. It is monotheism and Ma'at (conscience). In later times this religion was distorted and corrupted by Egyptian priests. According to the priests of Osiris, immortality could only be attained by belief in Osiris and the souls of unbelievers could not enter his kingdom, had no hope of resurrection, and, therefore, could have no existence in the afterlife. As a result of this interpretation, this religion was limited to some people only, and paradise was monopolized by certain of the faithful. The doctrine of faith became the doctrine of acting religiously, and good deeds, righteous speech and straight conduct were replaced by magical words, superstitious reciting and the sorcerer's amulets.

Akhenaten (1385 B.C.E.), a teacher-king, recalled the people to pure monotheism, but in order to keep monotheism clear and pure, Akhenaten ignored, but never denied, the afterlife. Perhaps Akhenaten ignored the afterlife because the Egyptians revered and worshiped the gods associated with the afterlife and to appease the cult of Osiris.

If one reads what was written about Amen or Aten, one will feel that one is reading about Jehovah or the Christian God or Allah. Aten, Amen, and other names—in Egyptian theology—were just temporal names, functions or attributes of the one and only God who is with no second, associate or partner. Akhenaten's major prayer to Aten follows.

Aten, the living one, the great one . . . the Lord of heaven, the Lord of earth . . . who liveth by Ma'at . . . who is great . . . the strong one forever.

Thou makest male seed to enter into women, and thou causest the liquid seed to become a human being . . . thou givest breath that it may vivify every part of his being.

How many are the things which thou hast created . . . in the face of the One God. Thou didst create the earth at thy will when thou didst exist by thyself, and men and women and beasts and cattle, and flocks of animals of every kind and everything which is upon earth and which flieth about with wings. And the land of Syria and Nubia and Egypt. Thou settest every man in his place and thou makest for them whatsoever they need.

Thou art the Lord of eternity. . . . Thou hast made the seasons of the year. . . . The earth is thy hand.

And the priests of Amen said of him: "This is the sacred God, the Great God who liveth by Maʾat (righteousness, truth and straightness). The one of one, the creator of the things which came into being when the earth took form in the beginning, whose forms are manifold and whose growth cannot be known. When He came into being nothing existed except himself. The prince of light and radiance. The mightiest of the mighty. He is the primeval water which floweth forth in its season to make to live all that cometh forth. He is the lord of life and giveth unto those who love him the whole earth and they are under the protection of his face. His name is gracious, and the love of him is sweet. He is the being who cannot be known. He giveth long life and multiplieth the years of those who are favored by him. He is the gracious protector of him whom he setteth in his heart."

Judaism originated in Egypt just after the time of Akhenaten. Some scholars consider Moses an Egyptian. His name is a part of other names—Thot-Moses, meaning son of Thot; Ra-Moses, meaning son of Rà, and the like. However, the name was shortened to Moses, as per Egyptian custom, and continues to be done so today. Whether Moses was an Egyptian or not is irrelevant. What is certain is that his language, education and culture were totally Egyptian and completely influenced by Egyptian traditions and understanding. Some scholars believe that Moses was influenced by Akhenaten's teachings. When Judaism came into being, the Egyptian word, Aten, became the Hebrew word Adonay, meaning the God, and like Akhenaten, Judaism for the most part ignored the afterlife. Judaism limited the personal significance of man to this life. And in the time of Jesus Christ there was a sect (the Saduccees) who did not believe in the afterlife. However, by the second century B.C.E., about eleven centuries later, the belief in the resurrection and judgment of the dead emerged.

When studying Israelite history, one can find in the era from Moses until Jesus a conflict between two doctrines—monotheism and polytheism, and a conflict between two systems, Ma'at (a system of conscience), and the ten commandments (a system of legal rules). The conscience (Ma'at) was neither put into nor expressed in legal rules.

First let us look at the concepts of monotheism and polytheism. Though monotheism eventually prevailed in Judaism, still Judaism reflects an admixture of both monotheism and polytheism. For example, in Judaism, monotheism means that the community has one God, called either Jehovah or Elohim, but it does not negate that other communities have their own Gods. Thus there is monotheism in the Jewish faith and polytheism in the rest of the universe. In the later books of the Old Testament, specifically the books of Isaiah, Daniel and Malachi, God is considered the God of all people, all of humanity. However, polytheism raises its head in the Jewish concept of "the chosen people," which means that the God of the Jews (because He is theirs only) prefers the Jews to any other people, regardless of their faith, actions and deeds, and for no other reason but tribal preference.

In terms of conscience (Ma'at) versus legal rules, Jewish rabbis misunderstood the positive expression of the conscience in the ten commandments. They found it easier to rule the people through religious legal rules rather than to educate them and raise and promote the individual and the collective conscience. Legal rules in the Old Testament and in the Talmud (the Rabbinical writings forming the basis of Judaism) became the divine instrument to lead the people, thus making them willing to obey, not to choose; to follow, and not to decide.

Despite the dissimilarities, there is much congruence between Egyptian thought and Judaism, from which we can select.

(1) The Egyptian priests transmitted to the Egyptians commands that they declared to be, and which were accepted as, authentic revelations of the will of the God. Later, all the Israelite prophets claimed that their revelations were issued by God.

(2) The Egyptians believed that they were the issue of the Great God who created the universe and that Osiris was to transmit his own ardor to those whom he loved and that his chosen ones sat on his shoulders. Later, the Israelis believed that they were the chosen ones (or people) and that they were the issue of God.

(3) Osiris was the "Great Word" in Egyptian mythology, and he was the "Word of what cometh into being and what is not." To put it otherwise, Osiris was "the Word spake words through which all things came into being from nonexistence." The same meaning is discerned in the Old Testament (Proverbs 8:22–31), in which it is said that God created the universe by wisdom (the Hebrew word is *hokhma*).

(4) Osiris as a God and judge must have held a similar position to that of Jehovah, who is said to judge among the Gods (Psalms 132).

(5) The words: God, Gods (Elohim) and the God (Jehovah) were used in the Old Testament in the same sense as they were used in Egypt (through the word *neter:* "The Lord God of Gods, the Lord God of Gods" (Joshua 22:22); "God of Gods," "Son of Gods" (Genesis 6:2); "Gods ascending out of the earth" (II Samuel 28:13).

(6) In Egypt the conscience was symbolized by the heart, and this symbol came to hold the same meaning in the Old Testament verses and in Jewish religious thought and literature that followed.

(7) It is mentioned in the Egyptian texts that Rà is he whose word when uttered must come to pass; the same was said about Jehovah in the Old Testament and about God in the religious verses that followed.

(8) Osiris was white and was the personification of good; Set (his brother and opponent) was black (or red) and was the personification of evil. In folk Judaism, Jehovah is white and is the good. The word *Set* was turned into *Setan* in the Cananite language (*Satan* in English) and became black (or red), the personification of evil and the opponent of God. The

same ideas infiltrated all Jewish religious thought, literature, and construction that followed.

(9) Much of Osiris' wisdom was imparted to his listeners in hymns and songs, which were sung, made into psalms or recited to the accompaniment of instruments of music. The same style was adopted in Judaism and what came after.

(10) Set attacked the sun god Rà in the form of a monster serpent or crocodile, called *apep*, the name of which is perpetuated in the Coptic version of the Bible (Genesis 6:4, Psalms 18:5).

(11) The Egyptians believed that the God kept a written account of the words and deeds of everyone, and a register of the years of everyone's life. The same belief came to folk Judaism and folk religion in general.

(12) The Egyptians' system of priesthood was adopted by Judaism. The priesthood remained with Aaron (Moses' brother) and his tribe, the Levites, who, as many historians believe, were Egyptians.

(13) In every Egyptian temple there was a place called the Holy of Holies. No one was permitted to enter it but the priests; the same was transferred to Jewish temples.

(14) The trial of the dead in the afterlife, and the reward of being with Osiris in his abode, became typical in the late books of the Old Testament and in folk Judaism and all that followed.

(15) The Egyptians cared a great deal about peace (*Hetep*) and praised the one who lived in peace, *em Hetep,* and spread peace. The doctrine of the Hetep became the same doctrine of the term *Shalom* in Hebrew, and Shalom has the same role that Hetep had in ancient Egypt.

(16) The Egyptian priests had certain knowledge by which they could use numbers and letters to predict or foretell many things; some of this knowledge became the Jewish culture, for example, *Zohar* or kabbala.

(17) The Egyptians considered their language a sacred language and letters sacred. They believed that the gods were speaking their sacred language. The same belief occurred in Judaism, where the Hebrew language and letters were considered sacred. As biblical language and as a modification of the Cananite language, the Hebrew language extends

back only to the twelfth century B.C.E. It ceased to be a spoken language around the third century B.C.E., although it remained a language of religious practice.

(18) Thoth was considered the messenger of God, Lord of divine words, and the Lord of the words of God. He was to make the word of Osiris true. Gabriel in Judaism carried the same function (Daniel 9:21).

(19) Osiris was the God of truth. In Judaism Jehovah became the God of truth (Psalms 31:5).

(20) Horus (son of Osiris) in the postmortem trial was the advocate and the intercessor of the deceased. In the Old Testament, God is considered an advocate (Psalms 57:1), and intercession became a doctrine in Judaism and all the religious thought that followed (Isaiah 53:12).

(21) The Egyptians would put all the sacred texts in a papyrus (or a book) with the deceased. This was called *per em hru*, which means "manifested in light," and is known as *The Egyptian Book of the Dead*. Later, the Jews also gathered their sacred writings in one book, the Old Testament.

(22) King Akhenaten used to pray before dawn and before dusk (just after sunset), because he considered the sun a symbol of the God; thus, he greeted and saluted its coming to earth and its going to rest. These two prayers said before dawn and before dusk became *Shema* and *Tefillah* in Judaism.

(23) In his prayer, Akhenaten used to kneel and bow (fall down in adoration), as is quite clear from paintings and bas reliefs. Prayer in Judaism, until medieval times, involved kneeling and bowing.

(24) In ancient Egypt the directives of God to guide man's conduct were called commands. In Judaism it is the same, as seen in the ten commandments delivered to Moses on Mount Sinai (Exodus 20:2–17).

(25) In *The Egyptian Book of the Dead*, it is said that Osiris is "the keeper of the book of that which is, and of that which shall be." The book in this text means the book of life or the record of cosmic events. This meaning infiltrated Judaism and all the religious thought that followed.

(26) The Egyptian conception of Rà and Aten as sun disks is very clear in many verses in the Psalms: "The Lord God is a sun" (84:11); "A fire

goeth before him and burneth up his enemies" (97:3); "His lightness enlightened the world" (97:4); "For thou will enlighten my candle; the Lord
my God will enlighten my darkness" (18:28); "He made darkness his
secret place, his pavilion round about him was dark. . . . The brightness
that was before him . . ." (18:11–12).

(27) Osiris was the light, as is Jehovah: "The Lord is my light" (Psalms
27:1).

(28) In a hymn, Osiris was called "Lord of praises," "he is greatly
praised." It is mentioned that "all give to him praises." Jehovah has the
same quality: "Who is worthy to be praised" (Psalms 18:3).

(29) In the moral precepts of early Egypt the God holds a position similar to that held by Jehovah among the Israelites. "Hear, O Israel, Yahweh
our God [literally, Gods] is Yahweh one." Yahweh one is typical of the
Egyptian term *neter uno*.

(30) Osiris was the man-god. This terminology also appears in the
Psalms about Jehovah: "But it was thou, a man, mine equal, my Guide,
and mine acquaintance. We took sweet counsel together and walked unto the house of God in company" (Psalms 55:13–14).

(31) In the late dynastic period it was forbidden to pronounce God's
name (US-AR). The Egyptians used to allude to him by letters (US)
without saying his full name. It was the same in Judaism with Jehovah.
YAHOWA are letters that allude to God but are not his name. In time
Yahowa was used as if it were a name.

(32) After prayer in Judaism it is a must to say "Amen" (Psalms 106:48).
Amen has no meaning in the Hebrew language or in any other language,
but the word is very well known in Egyptian mythology as it is the name
of God (Amen).

(33) In *The Egyptian Book of the Dead*, Horus was called after his mother
(Horus, son of Isis). In the Talmud, Jesus, in the same way, is called after
his mother (son of Mariam). In the Qur'ān, Jesus is mentioned many
times as "Jesus, son of Mariam."

(34) God in ancient Egypt was the father and the father of the fathers.
In Judaism God is also referred to as the father.

(35) It was a religious rite that every king be anointed by the high priest before ascending the throne. Anointing had the same meaning in Judaism. The word *anointed* (Psalms 2:2) is translated as Messiah in Hebrew, which means anointed generally but in this case anointed by God.

(36) After the fall of the old kingdom in Egypt, the Egyptians were looking for a savior to reestablish the golden age. Iepor and Neferroho (2000 B.C.E.) are very famous for preaching this call. What was written in the Old Testament about the savior almost exactly reflects the same words of Iepor and Neferroho. Neferroho alluded to the savior by the term *son of man*. The same term was used in the Book of Daniel about the savior, and Jesus Christ himself used the term when speaking about himself.

(37) The Egyptians used to say "the face of God," probably because they were alluding to the sun or to the man-god. The expression became a part of the religious verses in the Old Testament (Psalms 30:7).

(38) Circumcision was a very old Egyptian custom from the predynastic era (before 3200 B.C.E.). It is quite clear from the paintings and bas reliefs on the Egyptian monuments, especially those of Osiris, in which the organ is always circumcised. In the Old Testament, it is mentioned that Abraham was circumcised when he was old (perhaps when he was in Egypt or just before going to Egypt, since Egyptians used to despise the uncircumcised man). Circumcision became a testament between God and Abraham. After the Exodus, Moses ordered a collective circumcision, perhaps for those who were non-Egyptians. Circumcision became a main feature of Judaism and a religious obligation.

(39) In the story of Osiris, his opponent, Set, enters a pig while fighting Horus (Osiris' son). The pig then became the sign of Set (Setan, Satan, the evil) and the carrier of his soul or the spirit of evil; therefore, the pig became taboo. The Egyptians believed that Set's soul entered the pig either because Set's soul was dirty or because the pig is dirty and can cause diseases as a result of carrying the spirit of the evil. Egyptians never ate pork, never used the pots in which pork had been cooked, and never

kissed or came near anyone who ate pork. This attitude became a Jewish one, but without any explanation for it.

(40) In ancient Egypt, Thoth was the messenger of the God. Thoth declared God's words and commands. In the Old Testament the Angel of the Lord appeared to Moses on Mount Sinai: "and the Angel of the Lord appeared unto him in a flame of fire out of the midst of a bush" (Exodus 3:2); and soon after, the Angel of the Lord became confused with the Lord himself. The Angel of the Lord and the Lord became one. "When the Lord saw that he (Moses) turned aside to see, God called unto him out of the midst of the bush, and said, 'Moses, Moses.' And he said, 'Here am I'" (Exodus 3:4).

Although a verse in the Qur᾽ān says that God himself talked to Moses (Sūra 4:169), another verse assures us that God never talks to a human being unless through revelation, from behind a barrier, or by sending a messenger (Sūra 42:51). If one combines the two verses in a comprehensive interpretation, it will be quite clear that the messenger of God (his Angel) was he who appeared to Moses and talked to him, not God himself. In addition, it is quite certain from the study of the obvious two Qur᾽ānic verses that the word *God* is used in the Qur᾽ān as a figurative expression, and not literally. This viewpoint might explain many theological speculations. However, it is still unclear from the Old Testament whether it was Jehovah the God or the Angel of God who appeared to Moses. Was there confusion between the Angel of God and the God, in that the speech of the Angel was considered the speech of God himself?

From all that has been mentioned, it is quite certain that Judaism began in Egypt and was developed through much of Egyptian mythology, ideas and words. Most historians and scholars do not know, or neglect, the Egyptian elements in Judaism, looking for, and mentioning only, the Mesopotamian influence. During the Babylonian captivity (586–539 B.C.E.), Jewish priests took the Babylonian story of creation and recorded it in the Old Testament. Perhaps this was done in an effort to cut Judaism off from its Egyptian roots and sources and to mold it into an Asian pattern, since they were sure that Abraham and his ancestors were Asians and not Egyptians. But because the Jewish priests cut off Judaism from its roots, origin and source, much in it appears unclear, vague and contradictory.

At the same time, the Jewish priests borrowed the legal rules mentioned in Hammurabi's Law (1792–1750 B.C.E.) and put these rules into the Old Testament, as a way of replacing conscience (or the Egyptian Maʾat) with legal rules and to rule the people by religious instruments instead of educating them or raising and promoting their conscience.

Jesus Christ was, and still is, a revolutionary against all the distortion of religion and the slavery of humanity. In his teachings, Jesus stressed that there is only one God for all people, not only for some specific tribe or some certain people. He stressed that man's conscience should be cosmic and not limited. He stressed the spirit, not the words. He stressed the cosmic criteria, not legal rules. Jesus Christ offered a very simple and clear faith, with no formal temples, with no official rites and with no theology at all. He believed that every heart is the temple of God; that any speech, act or silence can be a deep and true prayer; and that everyone is by himself the truth, the way and the life.

Jesus' disciples and followers did not understand his very words and did not grasp the spirit of his teachings; thus, they created institutions and looked for a theology. Again, there are many similarities and much congruence between Egyptian constructions in Christian theology formulated at Alexandria from which we can select.

(1) Osiris was the Great Word, and he was the word of what cometh into being and what is not. In another text Osiris was "the Word spake words through which all things come into being from nonexistence"; so with Jesus it is the same meaning.

(2) In Memphis (Menph in ancient Egypt, about thirty kilometers south of Cairo), the theory of creation was that the God created the universe by

a word. The word—in this theology—meant the meaning, the wisdom and the action (as the Greek word *logos*). This meaning came to the Old Testament (Proverbs 8:22–31), where it is mentioned that God created the universe by wisdom. In Christian theology Jesus Christ is the Word; and by the Word God created the universe.

(3) Initially Jesus, as the Word, was considered an attribute of God. It is well known that in ancient Egyptian theology the Ultimate, the Absolute, the Abstract expresses himself in many attributes. In Christianity, this attribute became confused with the Ultimate (the God); then the Word—the same as Osiris—absorbed many qualities, potentialities, functions and features of the God. What helped the confusion is the lack of distinction between a god, who is any attribute, and the God, who is the Ultimate. The same confusion occurred in ancient Egypt with the word *neter*, which had the same pronunciation as a god and the God, an attribute and the Absolute.

The distinction and the confusion between the God and a god or gods is seen in the first verse of the Gospel According to John: "In the beginning was the Word, and the Word was with God, and the Word was *God*." The Arabic translation of this verse is: "In the beginning was the Word, and the Word was with the God, and the Word was *the God*."

(4) The story of Osiris deeply affected the Egyptians, who greatly respected the three holy figures: Osiris, Isis (his wife), and Horus (his son). In time, they were worshiped as a triad. The triad became a major feature of Egyptian theology, and it is the main feature of Christianity: the Father, the Son, and the Holy Ghost. Moreover, there existed early in the history of Christianity (until the seventh century) a triad consisting of the father, the mother, and the son (which is pure Egyptian).

(5) Osiris was the Lord of eternity, the king of kings, the soul of Rà (the God), the living soul, firstborn son, whose word is Ma'at (truth, justice and straightness), Lord of souls, Lord of earth, Lord of Lords, ruler of princes, prince of peace, great one. Most of these titles and qualities are the same titles and qualities of Jesus Christ in Christianity. In the Qur'ān, Jesus is the Word of the God and a spirit from him, the spirit of the God.

(6) In Christianity, the Virgin Mary is considered in the same way that Isis was considered in Egypt: Mother of the God (*Neter Mut*).

(7) The sufferings of Osiris and Jesus are very similar. The death of each at the hands of an enemy or enemies and their resurrection are almost the same. Osiris was life and resurrection, as was Jesus Christ.

(8) Osiris, in Egyptian belief, possessed two natures: he was partly divine and partly human. Egyptians thought that his human nature enabled him to understand the needs, troubles and grief of humanity, and to listen sympathetically to their prayers. They believed his divine nature gave him the power to help us in this world and the next. Christianity, in some sects, is almost the same.

(9) Osiris was the God-man, as was Jesus the Word made flesh.

(10) In Un (Ein Shams, in east Cairo today) the theory concerning the sun (Rà) was that it is *Khober* in the morning, which means "he who starts his work"; and *Rà* at noon, which means "he who is in his full completeness and strength"; and *Aten* at sunset, which means "he who has finished his work." This theory concerning the three appearances or aspects of the sun disk is the main concept of Christian theology concerning the Trinity—three in one.

(11) The cross, as a Christian symbol, is very similar to the ankh ☥, the symbol of life in ancient Egypt. If one looks at Coptic (Christian Egyptian) paintings at the Louvre museum, one will notice that the ankh was used initially in these paintings; then it was slightly modified by raising the upper circle, then the circle was made small, and at last the circle was abolished, and the cross took its actual shape.

(12) In the Gospel According to John, Jesus says, "When the comforter is come, whom I will send unto you from the father . . . Nevertheless I tell you the truth, it is expedient for you that I go away, for if I go not away, the comforter [in some translations: the advocate] will not come unto you. . . Now when he, the spirit of truth, is come, he will guide you into all truth" (15:26, 16:7–13).

If the word comforter is *advocate*, as it is in some translations, then Horus was considered the advocate and intercessor of the deceased during the trial after death. Osiris was considered the God of truth, which is so close, if not the same, as the spirit of truth in the obvious texts. Historians and theologians believe that the Gospel According to John was initially written in Greek, in Alexandria. The Greek word for comforter or advocate or counselor is παρακλετον, and its meaning is "he who is praised." He who is praised was also a quality of Osiris in one of his hymns and is, in Arabic, Muhammad. It is probable that the copies in the Middle East, or at least some of them before the time of the Prophet Muhammad (571 C.E.), had the word written in Greek as "he who is praised" and Mohammed, in Arabic.

It became common among Arabs of that time that the coming prophet will be praised. When the adjective became a name, many fathers called their sons Muhammad, wishing their son to be the prophet. The Prophet Muhammad was called by this name for the same reason and the same purpose, and indeed he was the Prophet.

It is quite certain that Christianity, in its pure and simple form, developed from Judaism as a protest against the chaos and confusion between monotheism and polytheism. Christianity also rose against the doctrine of the chosen people, against the literal interpretations of the Holy Book, against the tyranny of the priests and against the religious and political institutions.

However, because the teachings of Jesus Christ were not well understood, and the spirit of his words escaped most of his followers, Christianity came to reflect much of what Jesus spoke against. Jesus Christ was against formal institutions. From history it is quite clear that institutions were, and are, always dependent on texts, enslaving people and monopolizing the right of knowing the truth, explaining it and applying it. Jesus' true teachings were to free man—his body, mind and spirit— from any kind of slavery, to combine him with the cosmos, and to make everyone, by himself, the truth, the way and the life. After Jesus, his community consisted of a church to keep his teachings alive and effective. Unfortunately the church became an institution and sometimes strayed far from the spirit of Jesus' teachings. Christianity became burdened with instructions, literal interpretations, formal rites and philosophical theology. The ramifications of all this are that the Christian faith came to symbolize these philosophical questions: (1) Is the term *the God* one or three, by adding the two attributes, the Word and the Holy Spirit? (2) Are the terms the *God,* the *Word* and the *Holy Spirit* separate or three in one? (3) Is the Word the essence of the God or does the Word have the same essence as the God? And (4) is the Word with one nature or two?

Islam stressed monotheism and claimed that there is only one God for the universe and for all human beings. Islam refused any philosophical theory about the God to avoid what happened in Christianity. In the Qurʾān, Jesus is the Word of the God and a spirit from the God, but there are no theological interpretations given concerning this. In the Qurʾān, the God has many names, and in the traditions he has ninety-nine names or attributes, but Islam does not consider them each gods nor does it look for the relationship between the god's names and the nature of the Ultimate. Moreover, Islam carries elements from the previous general religious construction. Some meanings, structures and words from Judaism—the religion and the folk religion—infiltrated Islamic religious thought. Some of them became known by Muslims as a part of Judaism and are called Israelite thought; other meanings, structures and words are not known yet, but can be traced to Judaism and then back to ancient Egypt. Islam freed people from the clergy and religious political power to avoid what had happened in Judaism and Christianity. These are the authentic purposes of Islam, but the application is, of course, something else.

Actually all religious thought and formulas have failed to unite humanity or to give man right motives and true direction. All religious thought and formulas are insufficient to join man with the universe, humanity and history, mainly because religious thought emphasizes institutions and cuts itself off from its roots and origins and separates its constructions from others.

It is important to study all religious history, beginning from ancient Egypt, to find the common ground among all faiths. The similarities between ancient Egyptian religion, on the one hand, and Judaism and Christianity on the other, in doctrines, constructions, expressions and even words does not mean that Judaism or Christian theology borrowed falsely or incorrectly from ancient Egyptian theology. Rather it means that there is something common in all theologies and that, perhaps, the Jewish or Christian revelation may have been the same revelation as in ancient Egypt, or that sometimes the human mind can reach the truth of the cosmos before or simultaneously with revelation. Then there is only one humanity with one heritage despite all the apparent separations and regardless of all the seeming barriers, and everyone or every civilization or any theory could borrow from the Egyptian heritage, since it is a common heritage.

Making a sharp distinction among the three aspects of religion, it can be said that the ethical principles, the religious feelings or experience and the dogma (as a philosophical construction of the faith), are almost the same in every faith, except for a few differences due to time, place and circumstances. Every people (community)—Jewish, Christian, Muslim and others—has a wrong belief that the ethical principles are only for their community and that if they treat others in a good manner that would be proof of their own goodness. This wrong attitude would change if we realized that all the faithful are one community and that humanity is one and always one. The human being is more than the moment, his goals are beyond one life, existence is more than being, human potential is more abundant than an age and one's hopes are not to be completely realized in one's own time.

The authentic concept of Islam is that there is only one religion revealed by the one God to all the teachers, messengers and prophets throughout history and to all people all over the world. This religion, simply put, is to have faith in God and to be straight in conduct, which is the same religion preached by Osiris. If this is the essence of religion, to have faith in the Ultimate and to be straight in conduct, all the faithful in every place and at all times—from the dawn of civilization to the present—are one community. In the Qur'ān, "Those who believe (in the

Qur'ān) and those who follow the Jewish (Scriptures) and the Christians and the Sabians—any who believe in the God and the last day, and work for righteousness, shall have their reward with their Lord: on them shall be no fear, nor shall they grieve" (Sūra 2:62).

The authentic concept of Islam is that we all have one religion and we are all one community of the faithful. Every teacher, messenger or prophet had his own Sharī'a, that is, path, method or way in teaching the people how faith and righteousness should be lived in accordance with their state of mind, culture and customs. There is a verse in the Qur'ān which says, "We [God] gave you teachers, messengers and prophets of one religion, but we gave every one of you his own Sharī'a: path, method or way" (Sūra 3:84).

There is, then, one religion with many paths. For example, Judaism stressed the path of righteousness. It placed rights and obligations on everyone and demanded that they apply them strictly. Christianity stressed the path of love. It asked everyone to give and forgive without any limits. Islam stressed the path of mercy, which could be seen as a combination of righteousness and love, that is to say, you have the right to exact revenge, but it would be better to forgive; you have the right to take, but it would be better to give.

These paths never abrogate each other; rather these paths integrate with each other as the various facets, aspects or attributes of the same religion. We need each of them. Moreover, we also need the paths of other faiths, such as of Buddhism, which is the path of humility, and the path of Akhenaten, which is humanism. As history is one chain with many links, religion is one vision with many paths. The wise attitude is not to deny or neglect any link, but rather to deal with all of them in an integrated manner.

The relationship between paths, especially among Judaism, Christianity and Islam can be understood through Hegel's dialectic: thesis, antithesis and synthesis. It can be considered also as an attempt to avoid the confusion and distortion that happened in the previous path. It might further be seen as a deep and sincere action to establish the real and true system of conscience, instead of the system of legal rules, and to free man from institutions and religious rulers, either in the faith or in politics.

Religion started in Egypt, then appeared in many places and at different times. The result is that religion, instead of developing to its potential as a universal humanistic force, an element for gathering humanity together and a motive for development, largely became ethnic, limited, local, a cause for separation and conflict and a reason for rigidity, inflexibility and inaction.

A Framework for the Coexistence of Judaism, Christianity, and Islam: Common Thread of Salvation

I advocate a new humanistic base for the cooperation and coexistence among all the sects, doctrines and paths of the three religious cultures: Judaism, Christianity and Islam.

In Judaism, the Old Testament, or Torah, is based on the ten commandments and other rules and regulations that govern the life of the individual and community. In time, the rabbis offered new interpretations and new legal rules, which were set down in the Talmud. Torah, which originally meant "the way of guidance," was expanded to mean all of the juridical rules in the Hebrew Bible, and then further extended to mean the new rules and interpretations developed by the rabbis in the Talmud. Because the Talmudic law is considered all-comprehending, it is not easy for such a system to cooperate with or to accept any other system of laws.

In Christianity, Jesus Christ never spoke about law in any great detail. However, the church, after him, felt obliged to establish laws to regulate the activities of the individual and community. These laws came to be known as ecclesiastical law and are considered sacred. Thus it is very difficult for such a system to cooperate with or to accept any other system of laws.

In Islam there are many legal rules in the Qur'ān and in the traditions of the Prophet. Muslim scholars interpreted these rules and created other rules, which comprise jurisprudence. Jurisprudence is wrongly called Islamic law—Sharī'a—and is considered to be part of the faith. The word

Sharīʿa, however, does not mean law at all. Its meaning in Qurʾānic terminology and in the Arabic language is "the path, the way, the method," and the like. However, the term was extended by scholars to mean the entire Islamic system of law. Hence, this, too, is an isolated system that finds it very difficult to cooperate with or to accept any other system of laws.

These three systems, then—Judaism, Christianity and Islam—are closed systems. Each system considers itself an absolute and revealed system and refuses to recognize the other systems, which are, in its view, relative, were not revealed, or were falsified. How then shall we find a framework for creative coexistence among these juridical systems?

The solution, I am convinced, can be found in the authentic concept of Islam. The authentic concept of Islam—as mentioned above—is that there is only one religion revealed by God to all the teachers, messengers and prophets throughout history and to all peoples all over the world. This religion simply put is to have faith in God and to be straight in conduct. All the faithful throughout history and all over the world are one community. Those who believe (in the Qurʾān), and those who follow the Jewish scriptures, and the Christians and the Sabians—any who believe in God and the last day, and righteousness, shall have their reward with their Lord: "on them shall be no fear, nor shall they grieve" (Sūra 2:62).

Thus, in the authentic concept of Islam we all have one religion and we are all one community of the faithful. But every teacher, messenger or prophet had or has his own Sharīʿa—path, method or way—in teaching the people how faith and righteousness should be lived in accordance with their state of mind, culture and customs. There is a verse in the Qurʾān that reads, "We [God] gave you [teachers, messengers and prophets] one religion, but we gave every one of you his own Sharīʿa: path, method or way" (Sūra 4:84).

If we analyze the disagreements between the different forms of religion we will find that they are mainly verbal disagreements, linguistic interpretations and philosophical attitudes. People believe in words and differ about words, without having a precise definition of words and without keeping the faith away from words.

Instead of highlighting the differences, we should consider the common base shared by Judaism, Christianity and Islam, which is to have faith in God and to be straight in conduct. What differs is the path, the method or the way of each culture, or the interpretations of its scholars and faithful ones. We have to consider ourselves the faithful of one religion and to consider the interpretations and the jurisprudence as man's effort to realize his faith and to promote humanity. The absolute is a combination of all paths, interpretations and cultures. In the light of this, and in this way only, can we state a juridical coexistence for the three cultures and other cultures as well.

One religion, many paths, several interpretations, changeable law and flexible jurisprudence to suit man's activities without disturbing him or harming his spirit, his mind, activities, freedom and ambitions. Humanity must not neglect anyone because no person has been created in vain or without meaning. Every woman and man is the prophecy of the future and they were created to express a particular meaning, perhaps the one that no one else could express. Each woman and man's perfection and salvation can be attained only if no one is left out.

Along with the similar goals shared by Jewish, Christian and Islamic belief, these faiths also share the universal belief in salvation. Salvation, in religion, is the deliverance or redemption of man from fundamentally negative or disabling conditions, such as suffering evil, finitude and death. In some faiths, salvation is the restoration or raising up of the natural world to a higher realm or state. Salvation is a universal religious notion. Salvation may be referred to as deliverance or growth, and the concept includes (1) the basic goal of salvation, (2) the means of achieving salvation, (3) the cosmic situation which elicits the striving for salvation, (4) the notion of the soul, and (5) the ascription of decay and death to a primordial misdeed or to human sin.

The idea of salvation is traditionally associated with the very ancient and widespread belief in a deity (or deities) that governs the universe and that decrees laws designed to maintain a proper relationship between God and humanity, the purpose of which is to preserve both the cosmic order and the harmony of human society. The forms in which this belief has found expression in the course of history have been many and various. Salvation, the concept and the system, developed through different phases of history and through several stages of civilization.

In ancient Egypt, life was neither a sin nor a result of a sin. It was a grace rather than a curse. Salvation in this civilization meant basically not to be excessive or extravagant or to go beyond Ma'at. For the Egyptians, Ma'at had several meanings. Ma'at signified truth, justice, righteousness and good order, in both a social and cosmic context. The chief God of the Egyptians was regarded as embodying Ma'at—the principle of order in the universe and human society. The Egyptian concept has been the first in history to be aware of the relationship between the social order and the universal order and the first to relate the individual conscience with the cosmic conscience. Thus, any action or word against the society or any person or even oneself is considered a threat to both social and universal order; an assault upon the individual and the cosmic conscience.

As a result of these ideas (or perhaps a reason for them) death in the Egyptian belief was not considered a loss, nonexistence or annihilation; death was rather a way to eternal life, a way in which one could be eternal and immortal if one succeeded on Judgment Day. The Egyptians believed that a person's postmortem well-being could be jeopardized by accusations of wrongdoing brought against him after death. In the pyramid texts (2400 B.C.E.) are found an amorphous collection of prayers and refutations to all kinds of accusations, even those that might be brought against the deceased by animals. From the texts, it is clear that there is some kind of unity between all creatures and the cosmos: "There is no accuser (representing) a living person against . . . (the deceased); there is no accuser (representing) a dead person against . . .; there is no accuser (representing) a bull against . . ." [pyr. 386 a–b]. The implication that there is a divine law or order that the deceased might have transgressed is suggested in another text: "The deceased comes forth to justice (Ma'at); he brings it, that it may be with him" (Pyramids text 319, cited in al-'Ashmawy, *Development of Religion* [Cairo, 1995]).

Ma'at in oneself or in one's heart is referred to as the God in humanity, and it was evidently regarded as a conscious censor of the individual's behavior throughout life, ready to testify against him in the judgment after death.

Salvation, then, to the ancient Egyptians, was to pass successfully the judgment after death and to gain immortality with the God. It is clear and significant that the ancient Egyptians, while they sought salvation from death by ritual means, believed that the individual's eternal destiny was finally determined by his character. Salvation, then, was ethically and morally determined.

In texts from the tombs, the deceased would declare his uprightness, or rather, that he had acted in accordance with Ma'at and its ramifications. A notable example is on the tomb of a noble named Herkhuf. He claims that he "gave bread to the hungry, clothing to the naked, and ferried him who had no boat." He further declares that he never said anything evil "to a powerful one against any people," for he desired "that it might be well with me in the Great God's presence."

Salvation is the major theme throughout ancient Egyptian history. No one can escape the cosmic order and universal law of being punished or rewarded in the other life according to his deeds and his words in this life. Everyone, whether a king, a noble or a commoner, is subject to this order and law, and no one can escape it by any means.

In *The Egyptian Book of the Dead* (1580 B.C.E.) it is mentioned that the deceased—anyone—should enter the Hall of two truths (Ma'at), where he should declare his purity and innocence. Each declaration consists of a number of assertions of innocence of certain specified crimes. The deceased says, "I have not committed faults. I have not sinned. I have not done evil. I have appeased god by doing his will. I am pure of mouth, pure of hands. I am pure, my breast is washed, my interior (hath been) in the pool of Maʾat (right, truth and uprightness). I have given bread to the hungry, water to the thirsty, clothes to the naked" [chap. CXXC, plate XXXII].

Declarations were not enough; the deceased's heart (i.e., his individual Maʾat or conscience) had to be weighed, as was mentioned above. On one side of the scale is placed the feather (the symbol of Maʾat) and on the other wide is placed the heart. If the moral integrity of the person had been proved, and the assertions were favorable, he was proclaimed true of speech and justified in his protestations of innocence. In addition, rites were performed and pronouncements made for the deceased or by him in order to help him in his afterlife journey, to encourage him, and to preserve his body. However, these rites were never intended to prevent or circumvent Maʾat, the cosmic conscience, just law and right order, which watches everyone and rewards or punishes accordingly. With Maʾat as heart, conscience and God, salvation was to live with Maʾat and in Maʾat, to act and speak according to Maʾat as the individual and universal conscience, always strict, clear and fair, beneficial to man, society and the cosmos.

Judaism originated in Egypt after the time of Akhenaten (1358 B.C.E.). Akhenaten ignored—but never denied—the afterlife, since Egyptians had revered and worshiped the gods associated with the afterlife. Like Akhenaten, Judaism, for the most part, ignored the afterlife. Judaism limited humankind's personal significance to this life, and death was seen as the virtual end of a personal life; beyond death lay only the misery of Sheol, where there is no life. In the second century B.C.E. (about eleven centuries later) there emerged the belief in a resurrection and judgment of the dead.

A historical event in the early history of the Israelites was decisive in bringing about the concept of salvation—the salvation or redemption of the Israelites from Egyptian slavery. Due to this historical event, salvation in Judaism came to be understood as the salvation of the nation (the Jewish community), experienced primarily in this life. Salvation, then, had two connotations: namely, God's deliverance of Israel from its enemies, the classic example of which was the deliverance from the pursuing Egyptians and the destruction of the Egyptians in the Red Sea (Exodus 14:13); and God's deliverance of individuals from misfortune (Psalms 34:6). As Israel's position worsened in the interplay of power politics in the ancient Near East, the ethnic or national idea of salvation steadily became the major theme of Judaism.

In the course of history the Israelites were scattered. Ten of the twelve tribes were totally lost and vanished and many non-Israelites accepted Judaism as a faith. Despite these historical trials, Judaism adhered to its earliest experiences and understandings; it is mostly ethnic and nationalistic in origin and character; thus the term *chosen people* plays a primary role in the Jewish concept of salvation.

Salvation in Judaism, then, is to belong to the Israelite nation (community), to belong to the chosen people. However, this concept has its consequences. The eternal law of act and sanction—the law and order that was focused in the word Ma'at in ancient Egypt—is broken and circumvented by a construction of the human will that moves away from personal deeds and words; it is merely to be an Israelite. Despite the ethical code of Judaism, salvation, therefore, escapes cosmic justice and fails the universal order.

Christian theology was constructed long after the fact of the crucifixion in the first century c.e., but it was deeply affected by this fact. According to Christian theology, Adam disobeyed the God who had placed him in Paradise. The consequence of this sin is that he was sent out into the earth, where he, his wife (Eve) and all his descendants suffered death. "Sin came into the world through one man and death through sin; and so death spread to all men because all men sinned" (Romans 5:12–13). Through Christ's vicarious sacrifice, humanity was reconciled to God (Romans 5:10). Jesus Christ is regarded as the "Paschal lamb" that has been sacrificed to save humanity (Corinthians 5:7).

The main theme in the Christian theology of salvation is that by one person (Adam) death came to man, and by one person (Jesus Christ) death was overcome and life was given. To have faith in the crucifixion is to gain eternal life through Christ. However, no believer in this theology has escaped death. The promised reward of eternal life is shifted to the afterlife. Salvation, in this sense, is only for those who believe in the crucifixion and not for all humanity. What is more, salvation is merely a hope in salvation, since there is no evidence or proof that the reward is granted, or even exists, in the afterlife. Were faith in the crucifixion to mean a willingness to sacrifice without requital and to give without any return, it would be a positive motive to sacrifice even one's self without looking for requital and to give all that one can give without asking for any return. Moreover, salvation, in its current Christian formulation, escapes cosmic justice and fails the universal order by ignoring and canceling the eternal law of deeds and sanctions; and the rule of personal responsibility. Salvation will not achieve its proper meaning in Christianity unless it shifts from the fact to the meaning, from narrowness to openness. Then it will not be not only an assumption for some believers but a true fact for all humanity.

In Islamic belief, Adam's sin is forgiven by God. "Then Adam received from his Lord words (of revelation) and He relented toward him" (Sūra 2:37). Despite God's relenting and forgiveness, Adam neither returned to his first state of innocence nor escaped the result, which is death. His descendants, too, suffer all the consequences of sin and face death. Forgiveness and relenting means, in the Islamic sense, that man is not cursed with the first or major sin of Adam. According to the Qur'ān, no one inherits righteousness or guilt from his parents; instead, personal responsibility is underlined. "And who doeth good an atom's weight will see it then, and who doeth an atom's weight evil will see it then" (Sūra 99:7–8).

However, in the Qur'ān there is also a verse which may be understood as a contradiction to the eternal, cosmic and universal law of deeds and sanctions. "Had it not been for the grace of God (Allah) and his mercy unto you, not one of you would ever have grown pure, but Allah causeth whom he will to grow" (Sūra 24:21). According to this verse, salvation is a choice of and grace from God, not a result of humanity's effort to achieve integration of morality and action. In fact, interpreted in the spirit of Islam, the verse means that man should do his best—through deeds and words—to attain his election to God's grace. Salvation, then, is a mutual movement from the side of both man and God.

No Islamic text uses the word *salvation*, but some Qur'ānic verses mention "those who are saved." However, its meaning is contained in the word *growth* or the word *deliverance*. "O my people! What aileth me that I call you unto deliverance when you call me unto fire?" (Sūra 40:41). The understanding of salvation as a mutual action of God and man does not merely place obligations on man toward God but also gives him rights toward Him.

Unfortunately the Islamic understanding of salvation is distorted by the role of intercession. Although the Qur'ān (Sūra 2:45) pronounces that at the last judgment the intercession of no one will avail the guilty, nor can they be redeemed in any way from their fate, the Prophet Muhammad has acquired something of the role of a mediator or intercessor in the popular faith of Muslims. It is believed that God will accept the Prophet's intercession on behalf of believers guilty of grave sin (except the unforgivable sin of polytheism), and God will allow the Prophet to deliver such from Hell or to prevent such from going there. The Shī'ites hold that the Imams ('Alī, the cousin of the Prophet, and his descendants) also have this intercessory power. Moreover, in Islamic folk religion, the 'Awlīya (friends of God or holy men) have the same power. Intercession, then, allows one to escape cosmic justice and fails the universal order. Salvation becomes simply a privilege for some people—the best people—and not an obligation for all humanity to develop themselves through their own efforts, to reach out and take the hand of God, which is outstretched to save all humanity.

It is quite clear that since the end of ancient Egyptian civilization, most of the ideas and concepts concerning salvation might have been either misunderstood or distorted. As a consequence, salvation has been limited to particular individuals and communities or reduced to unproved ideas about uncertain hopes. Salvation has become elusive.

Humanity is from neither the earth nor the universe. It is *sui generis,* a unique creature. It is neither a soul nor a body; it is rather a cosmic identity, in which it is joined to both the earth and the universe. If—as a theoretical hypothesis—the human creature were to disintegrate, decompose or dissolve, it would no longer be human, but rather another creature.

When humanity was created through earth and on earth, its mission began. Humankind's mission was to achieve salvation for itself, for the earth, for the spirit and for the cosmos. To accomplish such a mission, humanity must control its will wisely, refine its character constantly, develop culture deeply and widely, and express itself with precision and eloquence. However, most of us allow ourselves to be affected by the earthly aspects of our beings and the earthly soul with all its negative qualities.

When humankind failed in this mission, it was captured by the earth, which is concentrating the negative (satanic) forces. Not only was humanity captured, but so was the spirit, the universe, the cosmos. Humankind, as a savior, needed a savior—the Word. Only the Word could save humanity, the spirit, the universe and the cosmos, since the Word is, by nature and essence, immune from the negative material and spiritual activities of the earth and can, at the same time, accomplish the mission of humankind and lead humanity as an example and ideal. The Word appeared in the history of humanity through every great teacher, messenger, prophet, master and inventor or creative thinker. The goal of the Word was, and is, clear and constant: to overcome all the captive elements within and around humanity, to draw the individual's attention to his or her true mission and to teach the individual how to act and achieve that true mission.

Initially traditions, customs and habits developed in order to help humanity. Traditions served as channels through which humanity could learn easily and quickly. Eventually, these channels became barriers, imprisoning humanity in past traditions, old customs and useless habits. The Word always teaches humanity to break out of the past into the present and then to the future, to use consciousness to tear down and then rebuild a finer edifice, utilizing the past and the present to achieve the future and shape it.

Humanity became very attached to its present environment and concentrated all earthly tendencies to separate and divide. Humankind preferred the temporal to the permanent and cared more for the family, the party, the community, the nation, etc., than for humankind, the universe or the cosmos. Humanity shattered everything, losing the sense of integration of one human being with another and of humanity with the cosmos. The Word, however, teaches humanity how to achieve equilibrium through an alert conscience, how to unite oneself with society through lofty ethics and solid morals, and how to integrate oneself with the cosmos through a deep and conscious sense of unification.

Man is a getter more than a giver. Since everyone is getting rather than giving, the world has become a jungle in which the main law is to overcome, to conquer, to defeat, to overpower, to overwhelm, to force, to compel and so on. The Word teaches humanity to sacrifice self in order to gain self. It is quite certain that humanity is a unity with many identities and that history is one chain with many links. Absorbing these truths will help in achieving salvation. Salvation, true salvation, is for all of humanity. It will never be for one person only. Unless the whole of humanity is saved, no one will be saved. Salvation, then, must also entail salvation of the earth (its soul), the human spirit, and the cosmos. Salvation will restore universal order and refine the cosmic conscience. Whatever one is doing or not doing, saying or not saying, affects all of humanity, the spirit and the cosmos and has bearing on whether or not we all achieve salvation.

The way to gain salvation is not only to have faith in God, in God's teachings and in symbols or rituals, but to expend every effort to realize one's faith in God, to apply God's teachings and to actualize symbols. A strong sense of solidarity needs to be created between people of every time and every place, to instill self-sacrifice in every conscience and act and to instill in every mind and culture the fact that no one will be saved unless one does his or her best to save the totality.

Moreover, humanity must act as a Word of God, that it act in such a way that one is the individual order for oneself as well as the universal order, that one is both the personal conscience and the cosmic conscience. If an individual does right and lives righteously, the individual will be rewarded, due to the universal law of actions and reactions, deeds and results. This law is meant to sanctify and purify, but not to lead any one person to salvation. Salvation is only for the whole, it is never only for the individual when he or she is cut off from the whole. The true and only way to realize and reach salvation is to feel, understand and live as *one in all, and all in one.*

PART II

Islamic Religion and Politics

The Relationship between Religion and Politics

Religion has been defined as the spiritual attitude of recognizing a supra-controlling power in life. Politics has been defined as the state of being organized under a particular form of government or similar institution. Comparing the two definitions, one can see that there is a correlation between religion and politics. Each pertains to the conduct of humanity and both are anchored in a particular power or organization. Religion offers the clergy—de jure or de facto—the opportunity to control human conduct and activities. So, too, politics is the work of politicians who control human conduct and activities.

The correlation between religion and politics began in ancient Egypt, where the king was considered a manifestation of God. In time, this understanding degenerated into a belief in the king as a physical son of God, as a personification of the one God. The pharaoh, appointed by God, was clearly not answerable to the people. He was considered infallible in all his doings and subjected to no one and nothing. His deeds were God's judgment, his orders were God's commandments, his speech was God's speech, his words were—every last letter of them—God's words.

Many historians have argued that Egyptian civilization became an international civilization that left its traces in many places in the world. With the rise of Hellenistic power in the ancient world, Alexander the Great set himself up as the god-king, tantamount to the pharaoh, declaring himself the son of God. In Rome, Julius Caesar attempted to declare himself a god or divine king. This action was the main reason that led his friends to plot against him and to kill him. The ancient Egyptian belief was suitable in its own time and place. It fit in with an entire construction of reality. But this belief is not easily transferred to another time or to another place.

After Julius Caesar, European rulers were eager to gain the prerogatives of the god-king or divine king, even if they did not use such terms. Clergy, in the service of the rulers, offered three theories by which rulers might attain the prerogative of the god-king: (1) the ruler is a manifesta-

tion or reflection of God; (2) the king's rule is the result of divine providence, which has arranged everything to this end; or (3) the theory of the
divine right of kings. Without going into these theories in detail we may
say that these theories helped justify the cruel exercise of absolute authority in medieval Europe.

Authentic Islam knows nothing of such theories. For it, no man—not
even the Prophet—shares in the divine substance. No one—again, not
even the Prophet—is infallible.

Throughout the course of history, the relationship between religion
and politics has been broken down into three types. (1) The founder of the
religion, the prophet or teacher, rules alone, formulating religious commandments and political rules. This is the case of Judaism and Islam. (2)
The founder of the religion abstains from politics. With the founder's
death, his followers set about establishing a church, an institution, and on
occasion this institution meshes with the political power, either to oppose
or to serve it, as happened in Christianity. (3) The founder of the religion,
the prophet or teacher, abstains from political power, and his followers
refrain from establishing any institution, resulting in the exploitation of
religion by politicians, as was the case of Buddhism.

In all states, rulers have tried to mold religion to their needs, veiling
their aims in religion or in the name of public interest. When a religious
institution sought to break free or to disassociate itself from the political
power, the rulers won out, protected as they were by the rich and the
powerful.

The classic example of confrontation between rulers and religious institutions occurred with Christianity. Jesus Christ refused to be a ruler,
judge, or arbitrator. His followers, however, established an institution
and the Christian society evolved with the idea of two cities: one the city
of God, named *civitas dei,* headed by the church; and the other an earthly
city headed by the civil power, *civitas terrena.* Under the feudal order that
grew out of this model, each prince ruled his fiefdom in relative isolation
from the others and religious institutions had the upper hand over all the
princes. Nevertheless, in time, when the bourgeois class was established

with the rise of the modern industrial revolution, fiefdoms gathered under one king who grew in power, supported by bankers, industrialists and traders, amongst others. The more stable the kings became, the more they used religion to serve their purposes, provoking tension between themselves and the religious institution. With religious institutions pervading and controlling every human activity by religious rules, the kings sought to counter religious authority by segregating religious institutions from the rest of society and governing society on the basis of civil order.

It was at this time that philosophers, intellectuals and writers created what has become known as secularism, namely the separation of religion and politics. Many decades passed before the sphere of influence of the change became clear, before the religious establishment was limited to the domain of religious activities alone.

The classic example of a religious community sovereign in both its religious and civil tenets is Islam. The Prophet Muhammed established a new system in which people no longer identified with each other on the basis of blood relations but rather on the basis of religious faith. The Prophet Muhammed was both the commander in times of war and an arbitrator of disputes put before him by believers. After his death, a Caliph was appointed in the Prophet's place. *Caliph* literally means the one who comes after another in time and the successor. Initially the word was used to refer to the one who came after the Prophet, but in time the word was used by Caliphs to mean that they were the successors to the Prophet Muhammed in all his capacities, thereby making themselves infallible. These Caliphs gathered in their hands both religious rule and political rule.

Since there are neither religious institutions nor clergy in Islam, the scholars were divided. Most scholars served the ruler, justifying all the ruler's acts, while other scholars boycotted the ruler's power and removed themselves from politics. Almost all Islamic jurisprudence avoided tackling the rights and obligations of the Caliph and his relationship to the people. Jurisprudence skirted around the public domain, restricting itself to individual interactions and social relations.

The principle of separating politics from religion, that is, civic rule, the so-called secularism, is needed. Politics should be practiced unfettered by religion but on the basis of civil code. At the same time religion needs to be protected from political distortion or corruption and unimpeded by earthly disputes or conflicts of power. When religion is meshed with politics it becomes an ideology, not a religion, and its followers become politicians or party members. To succeed, religion must recognize that it is a faith of profound power instilled in mankind's conscience to connect the individual with his family, society, humanity and the cosmos at large. Under no circumstances should rulers be allowed to exploit religion to justify their actions or to shield their decisions. Every action whatever its source—be it that of a president, minister, clergy, scholar or layperson—should be considered a civil, not a religious, action, even if based on religious commands. Since human action is the product of a human hand, it may be fallible and subject to the standards of right or wrong. Were such a distinction between religion and politics understood, religion could not be exploited.

There are three fundamental reasons why there is a movement toward sectarianism: tribalism, racism, and the religio-political dimension.

Human tribalism dates back to the beginning of history when the tribe was the only unit able to protect man and condition his loyalty. However, despite the progress of human history many peoples remain rooted in tribalistic ideas and attitudes. Most people are still enslaved by tribalistic ideas, which restrict them to one particular group, party, city or community. They live and act according to the strictures of their own tribe, and for this reason are separated from people outside their particular group and are cut off from the hope of integration.

Moreover, racism has spread as people are encouraged to emphasize divisions amongst themselves. Colonialism, in particular, played an insidious role in instilling such feelings. At the present time, we find racism across the globe and with prejudice nourishing hostile attitudes between different nations or within the same nation.

The most important factor, however, behind sectarianism today is the religio-political sphere. The religio-political element has perverted faiths into ideologies, resulting in the distortion of religious beliefs and a fueling of interhuman conflicts and animosities.

First we find that religio-political entities are ignorant of their own faiths and those of others. They know little but rumors or slogans about their own faith, and what they know about other faiths might be distorted shadows of ideas. The result is that they share little respect for other faiths, preferring to cut themselves off not only from other faiths but even from those of their faith who do not share their opinion.

Second, religio-political institutions turn faith into dogma in which the faith is ossified, closed and very hostile toward others. Faith is turned into an instrument for battle, rather than a basis on which to build and cooperate with others.

Third, almost all religio-political entitites deviate from the original, noble tenets of their faith. While most institutions cannot recognize this deviation in their own faith, they are able to find it clearly in the faith of others. Thus, they condemn others for being primitive, ignoble and paganistic.

Fourth, most members of religio-political institutions limit their code of ethics to the specific group to which they subscribe. The result is that each sect finds, in their relative ethical code, justifications for the murder, injury or extermination of others.

These reasons and others are in fact the natural product of transforming a faith into a religio-political institution. True religion, on the other hand, is open to all humankind, requiring each individual to refine him or herself and elevate his or her conscience to cooperate with all humankind. If we truly seek to unite humanity and flow with the movement of history, to gather humankind together and unite all people in one nation, then we need to devote all of our energy to returning religion to its original purpose—a means of interrelating, interconnecting and integrating human beings. This mission demands that we sever politics entirely from religion and restore religion to the pedestal of pure understanding, respect for one's own faith and the faith of others.

In the Qurʾān there is a verse that marks the dawning of such a movement: "Lo! Those who believe [in that which is revealed unto thee, Muhammed], and those who are Jews, and Christians, and Sabians—whoever believeth in God [Allah] and the Last Day and doeth right—surely their reward is with their Lord, and there shall be no fear come upon them, neither shall they grieve" (Sūra 2:62).

The Caliphate Government in Islamic History

The prophet's ten-year rule in Medina from 622 to 632 C.E., and ʿUmar's Caliphate from 634 to 644 C.E., also ten years, are exceptional periods in Islamic history because of the character of these men. The Prophet was just, honest, enlightened and under God's direct supervision. ʿUmar was one of the great personalities of history, likewise just, honest, enlightened and without any base interests. Yet these periods are very short in comparison with Islam's fourteen centuries. When we examine Islamic history we find that despite some noble models and despite the greatness of Islamic ethics, political authority has in general been against the people and has contradicted the spirit of Islam. In calling for an Islamic government, one must not allow one's hopes or wishful thinking to cause one to neglect the facts of history.

At the beginning of his mission (610–612 C.E.) the Prophet Muhammad was a preacher, not a ruler. It was only after his migration to Yathrib, al-Medīna (612 C.E.), that he became a ruler. If we wish to call his rule a government, then we are using the word according to its modern meaning, the exercise of political authority and direction. In the Qurʾān the term *government* refers to the administration of justice. To use the word *government* to refer to the Prophet's rule is to use it in its conventional sense, not in its strict Islamic sense.

In this foundational period of Islam, the Prophet received every legal rule by revelation and was supervised in his application of these rules.

Thus, the government in the Islamic faith was in this period truly the government of God, who had chosen the ruler, revealed to him the rules and their applications and supervised his every utterance and action.

After the death of the Prophet (632 C.E.), the Prophet's friend, Abu Bakr, became the first Caliph (632 C.E.). *Khalīfa* has two meanings: successor, and one who comes afterward in time. The first generation of Muslims used the word in its second sense when they called Abu Bakr the Caliph, since the office of Prophet is not inheritable. Later, however, the two meanings were confused in the minds of Muslims, and the Caliphs came to be understood as the successors of the Prophet and took on some of his prophetic functions.

Within a generation of the death of the Prophet, the Islamic state had become an empire and the Caliphate had become hereditary. The Caliphs and their court scholars stressed the view that the Caliph was the successor of the Prophet in all things. Islamic political jurisprudence came to revolve around the Caliph and his right as a ruler, giving little in the way of real rights to the ruled. The obligations of the Caliph, or the rights of the people, remained in the sphere of the theoretical. Throughout Islamic history, the application of these rules was against the interests of the people and the spirit of Islam. The rulers served themselves, their families, tribes and retinue. If the people were also served, it was by accident. Justice, wealth and opportunity were possessions of the Caliph and his ministers to be distributed as they willed; these were not rights of the people.

The Caliphate in Islamic history has always been a tribal office both in Sunni and Shīʿite Islam. The prophet's tribe, Quraysh, claimed that the Caliphate was limited to its members, and indeed, the Caliphate remained within this tribe for centuries. Despite all the vicissitudes of history, the Caliphate has remained restricted to particular races and particular families (Arabs, Turks, Ottomans, etc.), rather than being open to any Muslim. The debate continues in Islamic jurisprudence as to whether the Caliph must be a Qurayshite (many Muslims consider a non-

Qurayshite Caliph illegitimate) or can be any suitable Muslim. The truth is that the historical restriction of the Caliphate and the very fact of this debate about the Caliphate implies that the understanding of Islamic government as Caliphate is outside the spirit of Islam and contradicts those verses of the Qur'ān which call for equality among all human beings, regardless of nation, race or tribe.

For Shī'ites, leadership is centered in the Imam. The Imam must be a descendent of the Prophet, and specifically of Fatima (the Prophet's daughter) and 'Alī (his first cousin). Arguments about the relative merits of members of this family and to whom specifically the Imamate was passed on have resulted in many sects. Any ruler who is not the Imam himself is considered his deputy. This is the case in present-day Iran.

The Shī'ites consider the Imamate the sixth pillar of the faith. Thus, the Imamate is a specifically religious doctrine. In Shī'ite thought, the Imam is chosen by God and possesses a special divine light. He is therefore considered infallible—even though the Qur'ān does not consider the Prophet himself to be so. As for the Caliphate, it is not a specifically religious doctrine in the same way that the Imamate is, and yet it indirectly becomes very significant religiously, since its imperative is to protect and preserve the Muslim community. Sunnite thought does not, theoretically, consider the Caliph to be infallible; after the four rightly guided Caliphs, the Caliph was always considered infallible in practice.

The application of authentic Islam in the political sphere may be seen in the period of the four rightly guided Caliphs (632–660 C.E.). When Mū'āwīyya established the Umayyad Empire (660 C.E.), his capital was Damascus in Syria, which had been part of the Eastern Roman Empire. Because of this and because of Damascus' geographical proximity to this empire, the Umayyad Empire was exposed to a variety of Byzantine influences in both politics and jurisprudence. Mū'āwīyya and his successors were in need of theoretical justification for their place within their empire. They found the help they needed in jurisprudence. The jurists came to justify every act of the Caliphate. Since then, jurisprudence as it has actually been practiced in Islam has been answerable primarily to the rulers and has been opposed to the real interests of the majority of Muslims.

The jurists borrowed what they needed from previous theories of kingship, even if these were against the letter and the spirit of Islam. Their opinions afforded the Caliph great power over people, lands and money; practical infallibility; freedom from being answerable to the people; and immunity from replacement. In the sayings of the Caliphs and the opinions of the jurists, one can find elements of the medieval European theories of kingship. Sometimes the emphasis is on divine providence, at other times, on the Caliph's being successor, Khalīfa, to God, and so on.

Such theories of kingship became the basis for Islamic political authority and part of the Islamic heritage. The irony is that these theories contradict the spirit of Islam and the text of the Qurʾān. Islam has been distorted by this form of Islamic government and has become completely other than what it was originally.

Those people who call for this form of Islamic government are unaware of its true meaning and content; or they are ignorant of history, seeing only the political glory of the Caliphate, but knowing nothing of the social human and religious reality; or else they are led astray by the misuse of the word *government.*

To summarize: Whether by faith, tradition, religious reflection or practice, Islamic government, whether the Caliphate or the Imamate, has been centered in a specific race, tribe and family; the ruler (Caliph, Imam, Sultan, or whatever) has been made infallible; and this ruler has been given a free hand, full power and absolute authority over the people, the national income and the destiny of the nation. In domestic affairs, the people were almost always (with few exceptions) treated as members of a herd rather than as citizens; as subjects rather than as brothers in Islam. For example, the Caliphate sometimes demanded tribute from Muslims rather than the taxes they should pay as Muslims, as happened when the Ottomans demanded tribute from Egypt. Any sharing in decision making, any consultation, was completely optional and left to the whim of the

Caliph. No opposition was allowed, and when it arose, it was called heresy and damned as atheism.

The result is a sorry history of plots and intrigues, massacres and civil wars as those who had power struggled with those who aspired to it; for example, consider ʿAlī (the fourth rightly guided Caliph) and Mūʾāwīyya, the Umayyids and the Shīʿites, the Umayyids and the Abbasids, the Abbasids and the Shīʿites, and so on.

As for foreign affairs, it must be remembered that after the period of the four rightly guided Caliphs, the Islamic state became, in fact, an empire. The Caliphs, in their capacity as emperors, invaded other countries to protect their empire, increased their power, gained new subjects and gathered new fortunes. Many ethical questions remain, especially when we observe that these invasions were undertaken for temporal purposes and earthly concerns but carried out under the flag of religion and in the name of God.

Some would object that the main motivation of the Caliphs' wars was to spread Islam, but this is not accurate. For example, the Egyptian people were not converted to Islam until about three or four centuries after the Muslim conquest. In Andalusia, despite about eight centuries of Islamic rule, most of the native population remained Christian. While these are excellent examples of Muslim tolerance, they also show either that the spread of Islam was not the goal of these conquests or that Muslims were lax in their mission, and, in some instances, failed in it.

To give the Caliphs' religious support for their policies, Islamic scholars came to divide the world into the abode of peace, which is that part of the world under Islamic rule, and the abode of war, which is everywhere else. It is important to note that this well-known distinction does not come from genuine Islamic religion but is entirely an invention devised to give religious legitimation to the Caliphs' foreign policy. Thus, this division can and must be abolished to preserve Islam's true image, a religion of tolerance, equality and peace.

The Muslim invasions of Andalusia, Eastern Europe (by the Turks), and India (by the Moguls) left deep and hurtful effects. Many historians and non-Muslim intellectuals consider the rule of the invaders to have been cruel, arrogant and (especially in Andalusia) sometimes degenerate. They say that non-Muslims under Muslim rule were, if not persecuted, discriminated against, in that they were allowed to practice their religious rituals (under Muslim supervision) but not to exercise equal political or social rights.

The Caliphs and political leaders were wary of education and high culture, and often prohibited real education and limited teaching for Muslims to the memorization of verses from the Qur'ān, memorization of the traditions of the Prophet and memorization of scattered quotations from the jurists. The result was a high illiteracy rate, and the Islamic world's being left behind as the West steadily advanced with the industrial revolution and the development of modern technology.

Authentic Islam is aware of the consequences of using religion for political purposes and of using the people to secure personal and family interests. For there is not a single verse in the Qur'ān that directs Muslims to any specific political form or that ordains for them any specific kind of government. Were the Caliphate or the Imamate (or any other form of government) part of the religion of Islam, we should expect that it would have been mentioned and sketched out in general outlines in the Qur'ān. Nor are these forms of governments mentioned in the prophetic tradition. The clear conclusion to be drawn is that systems of political power and leadership are socially and historically conditioned structures, which ought to be developed according to the needs of the people and the spirit of the age and in keeping with the demands of Islamic ethics: justice, equality, humanity and mercy.

True Islamic government—after the Prophet—is a government of the people, a government in which the people freely elect, a government in which the people share, a government in which they control and supervise, and in which they may change peaceably, without bloodshed and without being denounced as heretics.

It was mentioned previously that in Qur'ānic terminology, *government* means the administration of justice. It is only by distorting the Qur'ānic meaning of the word and by understanding it as referring to political authority that Qur'ānic verses using the word *government* are used to support the call for an Islamic government like those which have appeared in history. What Muslims should in fact be calling for is not an Islamic government but a government that will serve Islam rather than use it, a government based on facts rather than slogans, on realities rather than dreams, on clarity rather than confusion. Islam does not recommend any single form of government and is absolutely against religious government. Islam is concerned with people, not with systems; with the conscience, not with legal rules; with the spirit, not with the letter of the law. A truly Islamic government will be one based on justice. This government, best described as a civil government, will come from the people and will be ruled by the people for the benefit of all the people. This government will gather everyone into one community and will exclude no one. This government will care about education, culture, science, art, history, literature and civilization. It will encourage cooperation, understanding, work, planning, constructive labor and self-sacrifice. It will understand Islam as mercy rather than as a sword, amity rather than enmity. It will offer Islam to all humankind as a way to God, a method for progress and a path for mercy. This is the new and true Islamic government.

The Call for an Islamic Government

In the Islamic world today there are increasing numbers of those who call for an Islamic government. They believe that such a government is the sole remedy for the ills of Islamic nations, that it will purify society, promote cultural progress, provide justice and exalt God's word. Others believe that such a government would be a religious (as opposed to civil) government, dangerously concentrating power in the hands of the clergy and their associates—whether scholars, politicians or civil servants. Such a religious government, they argue, would surely be authoritarian, based on narrow religious ideology.

Although there has been much debate on the establishment of an Islamic government, very little academic and scientific study has been
done on Islamic government. Modern political science defines government as the exercise of political authority to direct and restrain the actions
of the inhabitants of a particular community, society or state. Thus, government refers to the administration of public affairs, to the executive
power. In the Qurʾān and in the earliest Muslim thought, however,
government—*hūkūma* in Arabic—refers to the administration of justice,
while the exercise of political authority or the administration of public
affairs is referred to as *Amr* in Arabic, meaning conduct of affairs, authority, matter, principality, command, and the like. The distinction between
the exercise of political authority and the administration of justice is very
important, for Qurʾānic verses concerning the latter often have been misapplied to the former.

Why is there a call for an Islamic government?

The History of Colonialism

Since the fourth century B.C.E., there have been confrontations between
the West (first Europe, later Europe and North America) and the Middle
East. These confrontations began with the invasion of Egypt by Alexander the Great in 332 B.C.E. and the invasion of Syria and Persia in 334
B.C.E. Alexander's aim was the unification of the world by the imposition
of Hellenic culture, regardless of whether or not his culture was compatible with native attitudes and customs. Alexander's goal was not understood by many of the inhabitants of the lands he conquered. The inhabitants resented the cultural invasion even more than the military
invasion. Already, at the time, Middle Easterners felt that the West—
Greece—was destroying cherished customs and uprooting them cultur-
ally. This feeling was confirmed by subsequent developments.

In the second century B.C.E., Rome replaced Greece as the colonial-
ist power in the Middle East. The *Pax Romana* by which the Romans
achieved some stability within their empire was based on standing armies that could be rushed to any trouble spot and there efficiently and

brutally put down any revolt, root out resistance and quash protest. The real character of the *Pax Romana* proved traumatic, not only for Rome's subject peoples but finally for the Romans themselves. The Roman occupation of the Middle East left very bad memories.

Conflict continued into the Christian era, which is well exemplified by the dispute between the West (the Roman church) and the Middle East (the Egyptian and Syrian churches). The dispute is based on whether or not there are one or two natures in Jesus Christ. The Roman church insists on two natures, the Egyptian church on one.

After the appearance of Islam, conflict continued with the rapid Muslim conquests of Syria, Egypt and North Africa and in Europe, Andalusia (southern Spain), where the Muslims remained for nearly eight centuries (711–1492 C.E.). Muslim armies also crossed into France but were stopped at Poitiers in western France by Charles Martel (732 C.E.) The eleventh through thirteenth centuries are notable for the crusades (1095–1291 C.E.), which left the East and West with very bad impressions of each other.

The conflict continued with the conquest of the Muslim Ottoman Turks: Asia Minor, Greece, the Balkans. One result of these wars was that the words *Turkish* and *Muslim* became practically synonymous in the European mind.

In the late eighteenth century, France invaded Egypt and Syria and was soon followed by Britain. These two major powers divided up the Middle East between them. The English and French suggested that their Middle East policy was but a new round in the Crusades, and thus, a new chapter in the history of the confrontation between Christianity and Islam.

Two types of liberation movements arose among Muslims in the occupied Middle East: (1) a liberal movement calling for the establishment of a new civilization based on humanistic culture, education and freedom; and (2) an Islamic movement calling for the reestablishment of the Caliphate (especially after its abolition in 1924) and a truly Islamic government. The Islamic movement believes an Islamic government is the only way to unite the Muslim world and to defend it against the attacks of the West.

The Establishment of the State of Pakistan

Invasions of the Indian subcontinent by Central Asian Muslims (the Moguls) began in the eleventh century, and by the thirteenth century, a Muslim state in the subcontinent (the Delhi Sultanate) had been founded. These Central Asian Muslims were warriors by nature and possessed little of the real spirit of Islam, as is seen from their harsh treatment of conquered peoples. The original Muslims usually gave conquered peoples the choice of conversion or the payment of tribute money as a sign of acceptance of the new regime and as a pledge not to take up arms against it. To pose to a person the choice between conversion and the sword contradicts the spirit of Islam as well as the Qurʾānic texts that denounce conversion by force.

On the Indian subcontinent, the relationship between the Hindu (the majority population) and the Muslim (the minority population) forms a dark and disturbed chapter in the history of interreligious relationships. This is partially due to the great differences between Islam and Hinduism.

> · *Islam is a monotheistic religion, in which God can almost be said to be an individual identity. In Hinduism there are many gods relating to every aspect of life. If one speaks of the God, or the God of gods, one is speaking of an impersonal world-spirit.*
> · *Islam has no doctrine of reincarnation, which is a cornerstone of Hindu belief. Islam is a complete, well-defined closed system, while Hinduism is an open system, ready to absorb new beliefs, ideas and practices.*
> · *Hinduism is both a religion and a nationality. Islam is opposed to such nationalism (although some Muslims in the Indian subcontinent have not realized this, leading to the competition of two nationalisms within one land).*

These and other factors have led to a very unstable situation in which collisions and conflicts amounting to war have been common. Many Muslims called for an independent state, while the Pakistani outlook was characterized by defensiveness, a feeling of persecution and a constant readiness for war. Be that as it may, Pakistan is the first state in recent history to be founded solely on a religious basis. Pakistan has not only become a new model; it has also actively disseminated its unique attitudes throughout the Islamic world.

THE ESTABLISHMENT OF THE STATE OF ISRAEL

Until the last century, most Jews believed that their dispersion was the will of God and that by His will they would be gathered up again at the time of the coming of the Messiah. Zionist theory offered a new interpretation of history in which the will of the Jewish people should be exerted to fulfill the will of God, specifically by reestablishing the Jewish state. In time, the majority of Jews accepted this interpretation. In fact it has become part of the Jewish faith.

The state of Israel established itself in Palestine, a country where Muslims were in the majority. The Jews, however, believed that they were fulfilling God's promise, whereas the Muslims believed that the establishment of the state of Israel on their land, from which they had been driven, was against God's justice. Thus, the confrontation between Jews and Muslims took on a religious dimension, with God's promise on one side and God's justice on the other.

Within an hour of the declaration of the state of Israel on May 15, 1948, both the United States and the Soviet Union announced their recognition of the new Israeli state (although later the Soviet Union dissimulated her recognition in order to gain the support of the Arabs). Israeli propaganda and Western (especially American) actions convinced many Muslims that the establishment of the state of Israel represented a new chapter in the Crusades and a bridge for Western colonization of the Middle East.

The establishment of the state of Israel became a new chapter in the series of Arab defeats suffered at Western and Israeli hands. Hence, many have called for an Islamic government that would finally gain victory for the Arabs and for the Muslims. The consequence of the establishment of

Israel and especially of its capture of Jerusalem caused the strengthening of Arab nationalism and its transformation into Islamic nationalism.

Military and Semimilitary Governments

Most countries where Muslims are in the majority are ruled by military or semimilitary governments. It is characteristic of such governments to create permanent external threats by which they can draw the attention of the people away from the regime and thus reduce the possibility of a revolution or coup d'état. They typically suppress any sort of liberal movement. For the Islamic world, Western colonization and the state of Israel are permanent, external threats; and Muslim distrust of the West has been intentionally exploited and exacerbated. In the absence of free expression, there are no moderate channels for the control of emotions thus aroused, and Muslims are driven either to the extreme left or to the extreme right. The extreme left is considered synonymous with communism and is not popular in the Islamic world. So Muslim emotions find expression in the extreme right, religious extremism.

Corruption

In all times, in every place, in every society and in every community, corruption has been and is a reality. What varies is not the existence of corruption but its degree and kind. In the Islamic world the existence of totalitarian regimes and the lack of independent accounting have resulted in a situation where rulers may, with impunity, make use of public funds and foreign subsidies for their own profit. A wave of corruption results. While freedom, education and accountability are the true remedy for such a situation, many believe that the establishment of an Islamic government would be a sufficient cure.

The Decline of the West

Since Oswald Spengler published his *The Decline of the West* in 1918, this title has become part of the everyday speech of people all over the world. Usually the expression is not used in a precise way but as an expression of hostility or wishful thinking. The decline of the West will never automatically produce the rise of the East or of the Islamic world in particular; such a rise is dependent on factors and techniques that may be discerned from the rise of Islamic civilization during the first four Islamic centuries. Nonetheless, many people in the Islamic world use the phrase "the decline of the West" as a slogan for their expectation that the Islamic world, ruled by truly Islamic governments, will inherit the mantle of civilization being cast off by the West.

FLOW OF OIL

Since the 1930s, countries of the Islamic world have become the world's greatest producers of oil and the major suppliers of oil to the industrial nations of the West and Far East. In the 1970s (particularly after the 1973 war) the price of this oil increased sevenfold, and the producing nations became very rich. Since money in our current economic system means power (and since oil is quite literally a source of power), the power of the oil-producing countries was vastly increased. These nations quickly became important players in the international political system and have been able to promote (and impose) their own national identities, usually identified in some way with Islam.

Some of the Muslim oil-producing countries are prepared to support any movement, group, party, bank or government that professes an Islamic government or an Islamic system, regardless of whether or not there is any substance to the movement. It is the adjective *Islamic* that is important. These countries find their own identity in Islam, and the spread of Islamic systems adds to their power and influence.

TECHNOLOGICAL FRUSTRATION

Modern science and industry have led to the development of a very sophisticated technology. The West (the United States, in particular) has been reluctant to share the secrets of technology, preferring to export products rather than techniques to the Third World, including the Islamic world. Technology has become a new genie, something taboo, kept in a box, the sole key of which is in the hands of the West. The people of the Third World are thus merely consumers of the products of this technology but have no share in the production. Also many Third World educational systems have not been of a kind to prepare the people to develop new techniques or to share in production. Reform of educational programs is a must if future generations are to be able to absorb and then produce new technologies.

Consumption without production has the psychological effect of leading to passive and dull behavioral characteristics. However, most Third World people attribute these characteristics to the products of technology rather than to their lack of access to the means of production. Thus, for example, negative behavioral characteristics are said to be the result of watching television and videos. What is not noted is that the mentality, morals, personality and conduct of one who shares in the production of the television set or video are totally different from those of one who is solely a consumer.

For reasons such as these, technology has become a curse to the Islamic world. An Islamic government is widely regarded as the savior from this curse, perhaps because it is believed that such a government will lead the people back in time to the Golden Age of Islam, a period long, long before the curse of technology.

INCREASING DISORDER IN INTERNATIONAL SOCIETY

Since the 1960s, there has been a marked shift from order to disorder in international society. There are wars everywhere in the world, some of them civil wars. Newspapers, radio and television provide people with detailed and pictorial accounts of these conflicts. Terrorism is spreading and may strike anywhere and at any time. It is never more than a step away, threatening life, security and values. Separatist movements are endemic, threatening the integrity of many nations. One result of all this disorder is emotional insecurity. Sometimes the reaction to this insecurity is religious. The security and integration so lacking in the world may be sought in one's religious faith. This reaction is common in the Islamic world, where Islamic government has become a catchword for those who wish Muslims to separate themselves from a world in which they feel themselves strangers, and to create, instead, a new nation providing identity, security and hope.

It is conceivable that these feelings of insecurity might be channeled and developed in productive ways, which might even bring about a spiritual revolution. Unfortunately, what has in fact happened is that emphasis has been placed on external appearances, and the results have been nationalism and formalism.

SEXUAL BEHAVIOR

The sexual behavior of the West differs from that of the East. In the Islamic countries of the Middle East it is not permissible to speak of any sexual relationship outside of marriage (which is not to say that this does not occur), while in the West there is little such reluctance. Western thought about sex is changing; it is no longer simply a biological function but a physical and psychological human need requiring fulfillment. Most Muslims reject Western sexual attitudes, especially because these attitudes do not appear to Muslims to be grounded in or guided by any theoretical principles. Even those who have a more sophisticated view of sexuality fear the effect of such a view on the old conventions. Many Muslims simply look upon Western sexual behavior as degenerate and a result of Western Christianity or Jewish faith. In fact, the Western attitude toward sex is the fruit of Western civilization, resulting from Western conventions and character. Every civilization is characterized by certain behaviors, including sexual behavior. In Andalusia, under Arab rule, Christians blamed Muslims for the decline of morals, just as Muslims are now blaming the Christian West. Many Muslims see an Islamic government as the only defense against what they see as Western degeneracy.

THE IMAMATE IN IRAN

The 1979 revolution that toppled the Shah and his regime led to the establishment of what has been called an Islamic government. This government faces various problems, since it does not have the capacity to renew Islamic thought and systems in such a way as to support a modern state.

In spite of this, the establishment of an Islamic government has fired the hopes of Muslims hoping to create other such governments.

While the Iranian Imamate state may be suitable for Shīʿite Muslims, it is clearly unsuitable for the majority of Muslims who are Sunnis. In spite of the differences between Shīʿite and Sunni Islam, the Iranian Imamate proposes to export its revolution to all parts of the Muslim world, considering its government a model for Islamic government in general. Some see this as a Shīʿite attempt to overcome the old differences between Shīʿite and Sunni but in the interest of the former.

From these indications of the reasons behind the growing call for Islamic government, one can see that the term *Islamic* not clearly defined. Everyone uses the term according to his or her own interpretation, hopes and understanding. Many people in the West see in the term a sword being raised up against non-Muslims. For many in the Islamic world the term excites an emotional reaction compounded of wishful thinking, great respect for the era of the Prophet and the rightly guided Caliphs, a tendency to hallow the past and a general lack of knowledge of the history of humanity. A clear understanding is lacking, and the words are frequently misused. But most will agree that the term refers to a system in which Islamic law, Sharīʿa, is applied, and in which, whether in fulfillment of doctrine or simply in fact, a religious leadership controls the government.

We may now ask the following questions.

If an Islamic government is based on justice and morality and aims to spread faith, what may be said of other governments with the same base and the same aims?

If a government is based on equity and practices justice, is it Islamic? Or against Islam?

If a government aims to spread faith, is it Islamic? Or against Islam?

In fact, no government can rule unless it calls for justice, is consonant with some kind of ethical system and, apart from the atheist countries, respects faith of some kind.

A saying of the Prophet is: A kingdom may be built on heresy, but never on injustice. In other words, any government that lasts must be based on justice. In every nation of the world throughout history, constitutions and legal rules aim at providing justice. The problem, of course, is in the application. Actually political systems should be evaluated on the basis of facts, not on the basis of ethical claims that were never considered in the application and never made effective in history.

If the goal of an Islamic government can be defined as the application of Sharīʿa, serious academic studies must take place in order to explain Sharīʿa in a precise way: What does Sharīʿa mean? It is important to note that the way the term Sharīʿa is used today is not the way the word is used in the Qurʾān and does not correspond to its original Arabic meaning.

· *Sharīʿa (Islamic law) means the path, the method or the way.*

· *The path of Islam is mercy.*

· *To restrict Islam as a nationalism is to leave the absolute for the relative and abandon religion for chauvinism.*

· *To limit the path in legal rules and jurisprudence is to localize it in place and fix it in time.*

· *To confine the method in some texts and opinions is to fossilize it in words and nothing but words.*

· *Mercy is to have no confrontation with any country or enmity with any people.*

· *Mercy is to recognize and respect any other path: Judaism, Christianity, Buddhism, Hinduism, and so on.*

· *Mercy is to cooperate with everyone regardless of faith, color, language and origin.*

· *Mercy is to establish a new method of comprehension, to understand and to respect each other.*

· *Mercy is to care for humankind and to gather the past, the present and the future in one humanistic vision.*

- *Mercy is to look for what is human, not for the text, to look for the spirit of the text, not the letter of the text.*
- *Mercy is to spread prosperity, liberty, equality, justice and love, not only for Muslims but also for everyone, anytime and anywhere.*

Today Sharīʿa has come to include the whole body of legal rules developed in Islamic history, with all interpretations and opinions of the legal scholars, that is, jurisprudence. Therefore, in reality, to apply Sharīʿa means to codify Islamic jurisprudence. Muslims who call for applying Sharīʿa justify their call for this application with examples from the period of the Prophet (610–632 C.E.) or of ʿUmar, the second Caliph (634–644 C.E.), often confusing legal and judicial systems with the pure Islamic ethics of the early period or with particular events that are narrated about this period, in order to prove that Islamic government is just and ethical.

The Call for an Islamic Constitution in the State of Egypt

On March 3, 1924, Kemal Ataturk of Turkey abolished the Caliphate, the post of the titular head to temporal Islam, leaving a vacuum which every royal family and Muslim leader has sought to fill. One of the first to do so was King Fūad of Egypt. In the drafting of the first Egyptian constitution, promulgated in April 1923, King Fūad insisted on naming Islam the religion of the state. Article 149 of the 1923 constitution states that Islam is the religion of the state and Arabic its official language. Article 12, meanwhile, stipulated that freedom of faith was absolute, and Article 13 stipulated that the state should safeguard the freedom of worship, in keeping with Egypt's traditions, public order and morality.

Article 3 of the 1956 constitution, promulgated after the republican coup d'état on July 23, 1952, enshrined Islam as the religion of the state and Arabic as its language. In the present constitution of September 11, 1971, Article 2 states the same, adding that the principles of Sharīʿa, or Islamic law, are the main source for legislation.

Until 1971 none of the constitutions were ratified by parliament or referendum but only by royal or presidential decree. For the constitution of

1971, the first to be ratified by referendum, 99.982 percent of the people voted yes.

At the time of the promulgation of the 1923 constitution, Egyptians were divided into two camps—liberal and religious. The liberals, backed by the democratically elected Wafd party, argued that Article 149 added little that was new, since it merely expressed a fact. Religious scholars, for their part, sought to turn Egypt into a theocratic state, and with their call for the king to head it, they won the support of the royal palace. The clash came with the crowning of King Farouk in 1937. King Azharis and most of the royal household planned for a religious ceremony while Nahas Pasha, the Wafdist prime minister of the time, insisted on a civil ceremony, fearing that a theocratic state would give the religious ruler—the king—absolute and unaccountable power over the people and the resources of the state. The Wafdists won.

The debate reemerged with the promulgation of Article 2 of the constitution of 1971, which states that the principles of the Sharīʿa are a main source for legislation. The terms were not defined, and the constitution was declared without a prior white paper or preparatory discussion.

While some took the term *principles of the Sharīʿa* to refer to the general principles of Sharīʿa, namely mercy, justice, and equality, others, including President Sadat, understood Article 2 to be an order to codify Islamic law. To this end, Sadat assigned numerous committees to codify Islamic law, a project finally finished in 1977.

In my book *The Roots of Islamic Law* (1979), I responded to the committees that had codified not Qurʾānic Sharīʿa but rather man-made Muslim jurisprudence. The term Sharīʿa, as used in the Qurʾān, refers not to legal rules but rather to the path of Islam consisting of three streams: (1) worship, (2) ethical code, and (3) social intercourse. Worship and the ethical code were not subject to codification, while social intercourse was primarily subject to an ethical code, and only secondarily to legal rules. Of some six thousand verses in the Qurʾān only eighty contain legal dictates, most of which relate to family law. Of the remainder, one rule concerned procedure, another concerned transactions (though its precise meaning was not clear), and four concerned punishments (the conditions for application of which are so stringent that they could not be met in practice and are better classified as religious sins).

In *The Roots of Islamic Law* I showed that Egypt applies the Qurʾānic rules of family law both for Muslims and, with a few exceptions, for non-Muslims, that the procedural law does not contradict Islamic law, and that Egypt's penal code was no more than the man-made criminal law of society, which Islamic jurisprudence sanctions under the term *tā ʿzir*, since the four *hūdūd*, or Qurʾānic punishments, are difficult if not impossible to apply.

These points were simplified in articles published in the semiofficial daily *Al Akhbār*, amidst bitter criticism from a scholar from Al-Azhar who was the chairman of the committee commissioned to codify Islamic law and also the minister of religious endowments at that time. The aim of my book was to caution the government against altering legal terminology as a precursor to a theocratic state in which the constitution would outlaw civilians from holding the post of president, turn religious jurisprudence into judges and recast the relationship between the individual and the state as one of religion, not citizenship, thus denigrating the status of non-Muslims to second-class citizens. A fierce debate waged for some six months. Fortunately Sadat heeded my words and aborted his codification.

At the same time, Sadat issued the Political Parties Law 40 of 1977, preventing the founding of any political party on a religious basis aimed at thwarting the political ambitions of the Muslim Brotherhood. The Brotherhood applied to the courts for a license to form a political party, but after seventeen years of legal wrangling, the courts finally ruled against them in 1993. To date, all political activity undertaken by the Brotherhood remains illegal.

While Islamists continue to call for an Islamic constitution, the liberals argue for the separation of politics and religion, with the exception of the Al-Azhar Mosque and the Muftī, which should remain under the control of the state, lest a religious front develop against the civil society.

PART III

Islamic Law and
Contemporary Politics and Society

Interpretation of Texts in Egyptian Law and Islam

The conscience is a natural feeling that controls human activities and harmonizes humanity with itself, society and the cosmos at large. Conscience codified is legal rules. Whether by precedent or statute, as in Egypt, legal rules are invariably codified, even those relating to personal status and inheritance.

Legal text, be it the Qurʾān or modern-day statute, is initially mute. It never stands by itself or explains precisely what it means. Legal verses, therefore, must be interpreted accurately. Prior to 1952 each law drafted in Egypt was accompanied by a transcription of the preparatory debate, elucidating every word in every text, the intention of the legislator, and the purpose of the law in general. Each law was also accompanied by explanatory notes, setting forth the aim of the law and its clauses, and highlighting passages of particular import in the preparatory debate. The explanatory notes served as a vital reference aid to lawyers and judges when it came to the accurate application of any particular text or law. Thus, differences over the meaning and application of legal text were reduced to a minimum.

The same system was also intended for Egyptian civil law, for which a committee was commissioned in 1937 and came into being eleven years later, after the abolition of the mixed courts on October 15, 1949. But following the army takeover on July 23, 1952, the government issued a vast array of laws designed to change the political, economic and social structure of Egypt. Almost all of these laws were devoid of preparatory discussions or detailed explanatory notes and were little more than a repetition of the text without interpretation.

The result is that the language of Egypt's legislation has become less and less accurate, at times deviating from accepted legal terms and skirting the true meaning it desired. The most important example of this is the constitution of 1971, which was accompanied neither by transcriptions of the preparatory debate nor by explanatory notes. Article 2 of the constitution, which cites the principles of Islamic law, and which is a main (later, the main) source of legislation, remains ambiguous to this day. While some hold that *the principles of Islamic law* refer to mercy and justice, others hold this term to mean the corpus of Islamic jurisprudence, and still others hold it to mean Islamic law. The failure to resolve this confusion means that the precise nature of the state of Egypt remains to be defined.

A further consequence of this ill definition is that the nation's laws are now frequently misunderstood and require repeated amendments. Legal tangles have mushroomed, leading to thousands of petitions before the courts, which are often pursued for ten to fifteen years until they reach the Cassation Court. Though this court is competent to issue an unambiguous interpretation, a huge amount of time, effort and money is wasted.

Many jurists, myself included, have entreated legislators to return to the prerevolutionary practice of minimizing legislation, while ensuring that it is well-supported with preparatory debate and explanatory papers defining the law's intent.

The Qur'ānic text was revealed over a period of twenty-three years. In general, every verse was revealed for a specific purpose, normally in response to a particular incident or question. These incidents are regarded by Islamic jurisprudence as the reasons for revelation, so that each verse has its own historical context. Without understanding the historical context, the verses cannot really be properly understood.

Unfortunately, this traditional method of Qur'ānic interpretation has been eschewed by the militants, who reject analysis for mere literal meaning. The result is that the intent of Qur'ānic revelation is distorted and its true meaning lost. There is one verse, in particular, that has created problems for Muslims in every time and place: "Whosoever judges not by that which Allah has revealed, such are the *kāfirūn* (unbelievers)" (Sūra Al-Maida 5:44). From this text, militants choose to read the word "judges" as "rules," since it has the same form in Arabic (*hōkum*). They then proceed to accuse of being unbelievers all governments and societies that do not rule by what God has revealed. This verse is the primary justification for militancy and extremism in all Islamic societies.

If the verse is interpreted according to its historical context and the reasons for revelation given, its intent would read as follows: "Whosoever [of the Jews of Medīna at the time of the Prophet] judges not by that which God has revealed [in the Torah concerning stoning adulterers], such are the deniers [of the rule of stoning]."

This verse was revealed to the Prophet Muhammad when the Jews brought two Jewish adulterers to him and requested that he punish them. When the Prophet Muhammad asked them about the punishment in the Torah, they prevaricated, citing a different punishment to that of stoning. On hearing this, a Muslim recently converted from Judaism informed the Prophet that the Mosaic punishment was stoning. Thus, the Prophet ordered the two adulterers to be stoned, and recited: "How come they unto thee for Judgment wherein Allah has delivered judgment unto them. . . . Whosoever judges not by what Allah has revealed such are deniers."

It is clear that this verse was revealed in response to a specific incident and cannot be interpreted outside its historical context. Moreover, the Arabic word for judges, hōkum, evolved in time to mean not only to judge but also to rule. Similarly, the word unbelievers, kāfirūn, which initially meant to deny, evolved to mean to deny God. Thus, though in the above context, kāfirūn means those who deny the Mosaic punishment, it has been misinterpreted and distorted by the militants to accuse every society and every government of unbelief. This is but one example of the militants' distortion of the Qurʾānic tradition for their own ends. There are many others. Collectively their misinterpretations have combined to form a militant doctrine.

I seek to offer a liberal doctrine of Islam, rather than militancy. My first way to do this is to explain the literal meaning of words and the Qurʾānic verses in their historical context, or rather to shift from being textualists to contextualists.

Islamic Jurisprudence

The term *Islamic law* is the English translation of the Arabic word *Sharī'a*. Sharī'a, in Qur'ānic terminology and in Arabic dictionaries, does not mean law in the sense of legal rules. Its real meaning is "path, method, or way."

The word *Sharī'a* was initially used by the first generation of Muslims in its proper meaning. Then it was extended to include the legal rules in the Qur'ān. This was expanded over time to cover the legal rules, either in the Qur'ān or in the prophetic traditions. Finally, the term incorporated legal rules in all Islamic history. Today, Islamic law or Sharī'a refers to Islamic jurisprudence.

That which happened to the word *Sharī'a* also happened to the word *Torah* in Judaism. *Torah* means "way of guidance." Later the term was used to mean the legal rules in the Torah (especially in the Pentateuch, the first five books of the Old Testament). Still later the term came to mean the new rules and interpretations put in place by the rabbis.

As stated earlier, the true meaning of Sharī'a is the path, the method, or the way. According to the Qur'ān, each messenger, prophet and teacher has his own Sharī'a, (path, method or way) to explain and to help humanity apply the two elements of faith: faith in God and right conduct. Today, Islamic law or Sharī'a means jurisprudence, man-made and not sacred at all. To confuse this is to give sacredness to mere human opinions.

Today, there is a call to replace Egyptian law with Islamic law. To make a comparison between Egyptian law and Islamic law we have to go back to Roman law. From the second century B.C.E. to the coming of Islam, the Roman Empire was colonizing almost all of the Old World—Italy, Gaul (France), Greece, Turkey, Syria, the north of the Arabian peninsula, North Africa and Egypt. At that time, the Roman Empire had two legal systems, one for Rome (*Jus Civilen*), and one for the cities that were colonized, either in Italy or abroad (*Jus Gentium*). In time, the two legal systems borrowed from each other, merging into one law. Justinian, the emperor of the Eastern Roman Empire in 533 C.E., codified the law in the Institute and gathered the jurisprudence in an Encyclopedia. The Institute and the Encyclopedia include all the legal rules, judicial opinions and customs of the Old World. When Napoleon of France developed his legal code, he borrowed from Roman law and added to it all that had followed since the time of Justinian.

In 1883 Egypt was looking for ways to modernize its judicial system and to codify its laws. Islamic law was not codified and is still not codified, and Islamic jurisprudence is amazingly contradictory. In Egypt legislators adopted French legal codes, especially since these codes included legal rules that are not far from Egyptian customs. These rules neither conflict with Egyptian customs nor contradict Islamic law. Yet there is a call to replace Egyptian law with Islamic law because Egyptian law was taken from French law and is strange to our customs. The call adds that present Egyptian law, French law, and others are positivist law, while Islamic law is sacred religious law. The militants believe that these laws are positivist law because they incorrectly define positivist law as meaning any man-made legal rule when actually positive law means to define precise, concrete rules, no matter the source, human or divine. This important definition is not clear to many.

Actually Roman law and also French law, from which Egyptian law developed, are not so far removed from Islamic law. To make the comparison clearer, we should examine Egyptian law, code by code.

CIVIL CODE

There is no real difference between the Egyptian civil code and Islamic legal rules or jurisprudence except on two points: interest and the contract of insurance.

Some Muslim scholars suppose that interest is usury, and so it is forbidden by the Qur'ān. Others say that interest is definitely not usury. Usury occurs in a relationship between two persons in which the debt is multiplied many times in a very short period, while interest is determined, by law, to be about 7 percent a year and is a relationship between fund and fund. Thus, there is no usury in a relationship organized and protected by law.

On the other hand, some scholars suppose the contract of insurance to be a kind of gambling. Life insurance is forbidden according to Islamic rules, because no one knows when he will die, how long he will pay installments and when he will get the value of the contract. Other scholars say that there is no loss for either side in the contract of insurance, that it is a result of economic development and it does not contradict or disagree with the spirit of Islam. They add that the retirement pension, which is taken by all civil servants and almost every employee now (including the religious scholars) is, in a way, no more than an insurance.

COMMERCIAL CODE

There is no difference at all between the Egyptian commercial code and Islamic jurisprudence.

CODE OF PROCEDURES

There is also no difference between civil and criminal procedures in Egyptian law and Islamic law. Furthermore, Islamic law and Islamic jurisprudence have very few procedural rules.

PENAL CODE OR CRIMINAL LAW

Punishments, in Islamic law, are based on three systems:

- *Determined punishments, (*hūdūd*), which can be defined as limits or to set limits to prevent people from committing crimes:*
- *The law of an eye for an eye and a tooth for a tooth (lex talionis);*
- *Tāʿzir, which can be defined as supporting or strengthening. That is, punishing the criminal is to support and strengthen him to take the right path.*

Determined punishments (Hūdūd) consist of cutting off the hand for theft, lashing for accusing an innocent woman of adultery, lashing for adultery, and imprisonment or capital punishment for highway robbery. These are conditioned punishments—that is, they are not to be applied unless general and special conditions are satisfied. The general condition for applying these punishments consists of a community of faithful. In such a community, we will have just officers, just witnesses and just judges so that the punishments will be applied in the right way, rather than used in favor of someone or against another, or under the pressure of an administration or at the request of a ruler.

The special conditions differ from one punishment to another. Cutting off the hand for theft is not to be applied if the cause of the theft is need. It is applied to one who has enough of everything and is living on the economic level he deserves. In this way, the punishment is no more than a call or a motive for the government to establish a just and sound political and economic system in which everyone can be safe, have his needs met, and everyone has the intention of cooperating with the community and protecting the system.

Other conditions are important for cutting off the hand of a thief. For example, there is no cutting off the hand for stealing anything from the property of the government, even if it be millions. In the Islamic mind, the government has no property. Government funds and property are owned by the community, and everyone has a share in them. Thus, one cannot be punished for stealing that in which he has a share. In addition, there is no cutting off of the hand for fraud, either of public or special funds; nor in the case of embezzlement. Cutting off the hand is carried out only after many conditions are met, and it is not to be applied in most cases.

The second Caliph, Omar-ibn-Alkhāttab, stopped cutting off the hand as a punishment during a year of famine. Scholars say that was the right way to apply the punishment, which means that the right way to apply such a punishment is not when people are in a famine or are in need. In 1453 the Sultan Muhammad, the Conqueror, who invaded the Eastern Roman Empire, stopped cutting off the hand as punishment because, he said, people, then and now, need their hands as peasants, workers and artisans; and it is much better to punish with another punishment, and not to leave someone with harm to that person and to the society as well.

In ancient Egypt, cutting off the hand was a well-known punishment. For example, the hand of the forger was cut off. That was a clever approach because the proficiency of the forger lies in his hand. By cutting it off, one was destroying the instrument that could be used, and had been used, to commit forgery in the official and religious papers. In Hammurabi's Law (sixteenth century B.C.E.) cutting off the hand was a punishment for one who hit his parents. In the pre-Islamic era, for the first time in Arabia, Walīd-ibn-al Mughīra, father of Khalid, the great Islamic leader, cut off the hand of a thief. Subsequently this punishment became an Islamic punishment through the use of Qur'ānic verse.

A second determined punishment (*hadd*, singular of hūdūd) is lashing for one who accuses an innocent woman of adultery.

A third determined punishment is lashing for adultery. To apply the punishment for adultery, there must be four just eyewitnesses.

The fourth hadd is imprisoning or applying capital punishment for highway robbery. This punishment is the same in the Egyptian penal code, namely imprisonment for the crime or capital punishment if the victim is murdered.

Some scholars add to these four punishments two more: lashing for drinking alcohol, and capital punishment for apostatizing. In my opinion, these two punishments are not determined punishments (hūdūd), which are limited to four. There is no verse in the Qur'ān that states one must be punished for drinking alcohol. Neither did the Prophet apply a determined punishment for consumption of alcohol. And concerning apostasy from Islam, the Qur'ān says that it is a "religious" sin. What is certain is that the Prophet never used this punishment. The Qur'ān respects freedom of belief and condemns fanaticism.

The second system in Islamic criminal law is that of an eye for an eye and a tooth for a tooth (*lex talionis*), a law well known and common in the Old World. It is mentioned in Hammurabi's code (1600 B.C.E.), in Athenian law, in Roman law and in the Old Testament (from whence it came into Islamic law). In Islamic law, as well as in the Talmud, the punishment of lex talionis could be dropped if the victim—or the family of the victim in case of death—accepted a compensation from the criminal. In Egyptian law, the charges are never dropped by paying compensation. The victim may drop his civil right to compensation, but criminal prosecution is owed to the community, and despite any agreement with the victim, the criminal will be put to a trial if the evidence is sufficient. This is the right attitude and should be the modern application in Islam.

The third system in Islamic criminal law is known by the Arabic word *tā'zir,* which means supporting or strengthening. Under this system, the community or the legislator could criminalize any act and legislate any punishment. In my opinion, tā'zir is the main and essential penal system, because under it we can place a punishment to acts that were not crimes when Islamic law was revealed but that should be considered crimes today, such as espionage, bribery, forgery, arson of buildings or fields, crimes against the state, abduction, rape, and so on. By tā'zir, criminal acts can be punished when the determined punishments (hūdūd) cannot be applied because of the lack of legal Islamic evidence. As a result, Egyptian criminal law, and all criminal laws in Islamic countries, are including tā'zir.

PERSONAL STATUS CODE

The Egyptian personal status code is taken directly from Islamic legal rules and jurisprudence. However, we must be aware of the fact that Islamic jurisprudence consists of a variety of schools and many different opinions. Few of these opinions have the spirit of Islam in mind and most of these opinions are concerned with literal interpretation. Almost all of them contradict each other.

Two systems must be explained concerning the personal status code: that of marriage and divorce, and that of rules of inheritance.

In the pre-Islamic era, men had the right to marry numerous wives. However, Islam allowed for a man to marry only up to four women and on the condition that he treat his wives with complete equity and justice. Since the Qurʾān implies that man could not meet this requirement, the right of marrying more than one wife is more a theoretical right than a legal one. Because the interpretations of verses of the Qurʾān were made by men, men took care of their interests and asserted the right of polygamy, while dropping the condition of just treatment.

By the contract of marriage, the man legally has the right of divorce. The woman can share this right, or may have it alone, or both husband and wife may transfer the right of divorce to a third person. The important reformation some Islamic countries established was to give the right of divorce only to the court. The marriage contract in Islam is a civil contract rather than a religious one. The partners could arrange its conditions together.

By the laws of inheritance, male heirs have double the amount of shares of the female. In the first era of Islam, the community consisted of tribes in which the men had responsibilities toward the women. For example, a man had to protect and provide for his wife. Thus, the system of shares was put in place to meet the needs of the people. Later, when Islam became an empire, tribes vanished in the cities and villages. As a result, the obligations of men toward their women diminished, and many people became disenchanted with the inheritance law. Because the character of Islamic jurisprudence is to search for an original and suitable device rather than to look for an individual opinion, scholars invented the system of endowment or family immobilization (*waqf*) to prevent family property from being bought and sold and to exempt it from circulation. According to this system, it is sufficient for someone to declare that God is the owner of his property, to have by this act of endowment the right of changing his heirs and determining the shares as he wishes, rather than according to the prescribed Qurʾānic heirs. Waqf is proof that laws are always changeable, and if they are not changed in a legal and clear way to meet people's changing needs, their prescriptions will be escaped.

Taxes, *Zakāt*, and *Sadaqa*

Every state, including Egypt, imposes taxes on its subjects in order to finance its budget and provide services that the public expects of the state, such as roads, infrastructure, hospitals and free education. In some cases, foreign residents are also required to contribute. In the most recent amendment to the taxation law, taxes were imposed on any profit or income earned abroad by either legal Egyptians or fictitious persons, such as companies or banks.

Yet taxes are but one face of the sovereignty of the state. Egyptian society, in the main, applies the Islamic view that the rich should give alms to the poor. The rich are not compelled to do so, nor are the means or measure of distribution specified. Almsgiving, the third of the five pillars of Islam, is called zakāt. Islam also encourages the donation of *sadaqa,* or gifts, but historically zakāt and sadaqa have been confused.

Some argue that the government should collect zakāt to increase its revenue and, hence, its budget, to provide pensions as well as welfare and unemployment benefits for all the needy on Egyptian soil without distinction of faith, color or gender. The present system, for instance, makes only partial provision for the retired, with a small pension known as Sadat's Pension, distributed to but a few segments of the poor.

The word *zakāt* occurs thirty-two times in the Qurʾān, but on each occasion it leaves the amount and the frequency to the discretion of every Muslim. The Muslim must only ensure that he is giving and not merely taking of the precious things in life and must give whenever he can. There are but a few occasions when zakāt is determined, such as the eve of ʿId al-Fitr—the feast that marks the end of the fasting month of Ramadan— in which the zakāt amount is calculated at the rate of two pounds of wheat per family member, to be paid to the poor by the head of the family. Zakāt at a rate of 2.5 percent must also be paid on all savings or jewelry held over from one year to the next.

Sadaqa, on the other hand, is derived from the Hebrew word *tzedeq,* meaning righteousness. The word *sadaqa* appears five times in the Qurʾān and denotes a gift entrusted to the Prophet either willingly or unwillingly. "Take sadaqa (a gift) of their wealth, wherewith thou mayst purify them and mayst make them grow, and pray for them" (Sūra 9:113). It is also mentioned in Sūra 58:12: "O ye who believe, when you hold conference with the messenger, offer sadaqa before your conference. That is better and purer for you. But if you cannot find [the wherewithal] then lo! Allah is Merciful and Forgiving."

Clearly sadaqa is a gift entrusted to the Prophet either at the behest of the Qur'ān or given willingly by believers. Only the Prophet had the right to spend it in ways stipulated by the Qur'ān: "The sadaqa is only for the poor and the needy and those who collect them, and those whose hearts are to be reconciled (the nonbelievers, those who are against Islam). And to free the captives and the debtors, and for the cause of Allah and for the wayfarer, a duty imposed by Allah" (Sūra 9:60).

While it is apparent that sadaqa is something other than alms, since alms are neither determined by nor to be given to the debtor or to those whose hearts are to be reconciled, the zakāt and sadaqa became confused in Islamic tradition. Both have been considered alms. Current Islamic tradition fails to realize that while zakāt means alms, or an undetermined sum to be distributed by Muslims to the poor, needy and old, sadaqa is a gift.

In the first era of Islam, when the rightly guided caliphs ruled, every Muslim was entitled to a welfare from the *Bayt al-Māl,* or state treasury. Unfortunately, during the Umayyad dynasty, from twenty-eight years after the Prophet's death onward, the Caliphs considered the state treasury their own private property and negated their duties to provide from state revenue on a regular basis for the poor, the needy, the orphans, the widows, the old and the sick. Instead, the Caliphs left the poor to live on the alms of the people, which may have sufficed in a small community but could not cater to the needs of a modern state. A way should be found to provide permanent and fixed benefits for the poor, ill, orphans, widows or elderly. At the same time, a system of welfare and unemployment benefits should be introduced. To do so would be to realize and apply the spirit of Islam, which calls for cooperation between people, while hold-ing the dispossessed or ill in high regard.

The Veil in Egyptian Law and Islam

Egyptian law sets no code for clothing. Anyone can dress howsoever he or she chooses. However, no one is allowed to appear naked in public places or expose their genitals, nor may women reveal their breasts. If this happens, it is considered a misdemeanor, punishable under Article 278 of the Penal Code of 1937 by imprisonment for a maximum of one year, or by a fine of E£300.

The law aside, Egypt's conventions have always required those on its soil to dress decently. Until recently, Egyptian women in the cities were decently dressed but generally went unveiled. Egyptian peasants and the urban lower middle classes would cover their heads either with a *tarha*, a scarf, or a decorated kerchief. After the heavy wave of migration to the Gulf states in the 1970s, women were forced to don the veil, and preach-ers and propagandists of political Islam stressed that the veil was an Islamic dress required by the Qurʾān and the prophetic traditions. Yet there is no mention of the veil in Egyptian law. Young men who sought to intimidate young women said that if a woman failed to wear the veil she was dueling with God. Many Egyptian girls donned the veil in fear, with-out questioning the real meaning of the Qurʾānic verse or the verbal tra-ditions that support it.

The veil is mentioned in Sūra 33:53: "And when ye ask [his wives] for anything ye want; ask them from before a screen; that makes; for greater purity for your hearts and for theirs." This verse applies only to the wives of the Prophet and refers not to a veiling of the face or a headcovering but to a curtain that had to hang between the male community of the faithful and the Prophet's wives.

The Qurʾān refers again to the "veil" in Sūra 24:31: "And say to the believing women that they should lower their gaze and guard their mod-esty; that they should not display their beauty and ornaments except what ordinarily appears thereof; that they should draw their clothing over their bosoms." It is quite clear from the historical context that this verse was revealed to modify an ancient Arab custom of covering the head with a scarf or veil and baring the breasts. The commandment called on the faithful women and girls to cover their breasts and not to leave them bare as was the custom of the time.

The Qur'ān makes a third reference to a covering, which is considered a *hijāb,* in Sūra 33:59: "O Prophet! Tell thy wives and daughters, and the believing women, that they should cast their outer garments over their persons [when out of doors]: that is most convenient that they should be known [as decent women] and not molested." This verse calls on faithful women and girls to cloak themselves with their traditional Egyptian dress, the *gellabīya.* It is not clear whether this verse refers to a veil covering the face or head. Moreover, it is quite clear from the historical context that this verse was revealed to separate decent women from the concubines of a slavery harem, these being common at the time. Nowadays there are no concubines or slavery harems, so the verse no longer applies.

In general, the Qur'ān should be interpreted not according to the general meaning of its words but according to the historical context in which it was given. For this reason, some Qur'ānic rulings are temporary rather than permanent. For example, the injunctions regarding the system of slavery and the slave harem were mentioned in the Qur'ān but abolished by legislators across the Islamic world. And the pleasure marriage, *mūta'a,* which is accepted by the Shī'ites on the authority of a Qur'ānic verse, is not accepted by the Sunnis, who say that the verse was abrogated by the Prophet.

Because Qur'ānic verses are not entirely clear about the wearing of the veil, most scholars rely on prophetic tradition to support donning the veil. But, again, the same problem arises: are the rulings found in the prophetic tradition permanent or do they have but temporary application to the time of the Prophet? Most scholars side with the latter view. Islam recommends that women and girls dress decently, but does not insist that women and girls of the twentieth century don the veil. They may wear the veil, if they so choose, but should in no way be threatened or intimidated into wearing it on the pretext that it is a command from God or the Prophet.

Today, veils, beards and gellabīyas are sometimes considered as signs of political Islam and as proof of the strength of its militancy. Jurists who justify the actions of political Islam prevent the issue of the veil being debated in the appropriate way—through interpretation of the Qurʾān and the prophetic traditions.

Militant Doctrine in Islam

Nowadays, the term *militant Islam* is a very widespread slogan, unwittingly used everywhere by many as if it were a refrain to describe Islam. Actually it destroys the image of Islam and implies that Islam is a militant faith and nothing else.

In the Islamic world in general, and in Egypt in particular, there are two movements: (1) the liberal, the enlightened, or the intellectual, and (2) the militant, the activist, or the warlike. These movements differ both in doctrinal emphasis and in methodology. The central tenets of the militants—who are opposed, countered and answered by the liberals—are the following seven points.

(1) Islam is seen by the militants as the sole, valid and complete faith, abrogating all other faiths. It follows from this that all non-Muslims are infidels and should be converted to Islam, even by force (*jihād* or holy war). In dealing with this issue, it is necessary to maintain a more complex position based on the real understanding of revelation, and the true comprehension of Islam as a path or Sharīʿa.

It suffices to point out that it is mentioned in the Qurʾān that God gave all the prophets one faith but different paths. Every messenger or prophet was given his own path. For example, Moses revealed the path of justice; Jesus revealed the path of love, demonstrated in self-sacrifice; and Muhammad revealed the path of mercy, which combines the paths of justice and love. In the path of mercy, revenge is tolerated (as Moses' path), but forgiveness (as Jesus' path) is held to be better. In this sense, Islam, as a path, did not abrogate any other paths and as such must cooperate with other paths rather war against them.

At this point it must be stressed that the Qurʾānic verse says, "God completed for the faithful [Muslims] their faith" (Sūra 5:3), does not imply that "faith" as such was not completed; rather it means that the rites (rituals) of Islam were completed after Muslims were allowed to go on pilgrimage for the first time.

(2) The militant's doctrine maintains that politics is a part of Islam, without clarifying whether by Islam they mean the faith or Islamic history in general.

This is an important distinction to make because if, on the one hand, by Islam is meant the faith itself, then the militant's position is not acceptable, for if politics is part of faith, then it is a pillar of Islam or a cornerstone of its dogma. Such a position would add politics to the five pillars of the Sunnite Islam, making them six, which is the Shīʿite doctrine. This claim amounts to undermining the Sunnite doctrine (which is the majority) for the Shīʿite doctrine (which is the minority).

If, on the other hand, by Islam is meant the history of Islam, then obviously politics is part and parcel of it. However, politics is not the essence of Islam. The legitimacy of a civil state (wrongly called secular state) has not been denied to Islam, nor is a civil state considered against or as a rival to Islam. Moreover, having a civil state would mean automatically excluding any religious party as an opposition, for it is hardly tenable to have a religious party as an opposition to a civil state. All of these elements considered, therefore, politics is neither a cornerstone of dogma nor a pillar in Islam, and a religious state is not acceptable nor is religious opposition allowable or a religious party tolerable. In fact, a religious state would in practice be totalitarian, meaning that it would give its own acts the quality of divinity, as if it acted with perfection and absolutism. Thus, it would demand passive and absolute obedience from its subjects. A religious party would also manifest the same characteristics and would always look to undermine the state, other parties and society itself. On the contrary, a civil state cannot consider its acts perfect or absolute or not to be discussed, because every civil act is necessarily human and not divine, thus neither perfect nor absolute nor immune from criticism.

(3) The militant doctrine perceives the ruler's acts as divine.

This ideology is fed to the naive and uneducated masses in questions and statements such as, "Do you want to be governed by God or man?" "Man will never achieve success unless he is ruled by God." Such questions and statements infer that the ruler's acts are divine and carried out in the name of God. Actually God rules the world in general, but in particular everyone is responsible for his or her own actions and deeds, whether positive or negative, whether done or said, or not to be done and said. In fact, the whole issue of divine right to rule is based on a misunderstanding of the Qur'ānic term *hōkum*. While the word means in Qur'ānic terminology "to judge" or "justice administration," militants have distorted and falsified hōkum to mean "to govern" or "a government." If God is ruling and acting by Himself, this would amount to the abrogation of the principle of responsibility, since every ruler could say: "These are God's deeds and governance and not mine." And everyone could say for every misdeed committed: "It is God's deeds and speech, not mine at all." Thus, no one would be responsible or accountable for anything, and no legal rules would be applied—not even the conscience would be necessary or important. In such an atmosphere, faith, state, civilization and humanity would be undermined.

(4) Militants do not view Islam as a faith but rather as nationalism.

Militants believe that loyalty and devotion to the nation of Islam, exalting it above all others and placing primary emphasis on promotion of its culture and interests as opposed to those of the nation and other nations, is a given, and anyone who believes otherwise is an infidel or atheist. Such a belief clearly misses the point. Islam, as a faith, is not limited to a certain nation or to certain people, but is a faith open to everyone all over the world. Considering Islam as nationalism contradicts Islam itself and goes against the national interest of any country. Considering Islam as nationalism also contradicts the Islamic faith, because it restricts the Islamic message to the few. Likewise, considering Islam as nationalism goes against national interests, because it undermines the loyalty of a Muslim living in a non-Muslim country and it cuts off the rights of non-Muslims who live in an Islamic country.

(5) The militant's main objective is to apply Islamic law. It is a Muslim's duty, according to the militants, not to obey or to apply any other law. Islamic law, in general, means the law of Islam, and it provides a method of dealing with God and man. Islamic law does not mean any specific legal rule or rules. Today its meaning has been changed to mean all legal rules that are to be found in all Islamic history and all the interpretations and opinions that constitute Islamic jurisprudence. Today, Islamic law means Islamic jurisprudence and the political system.

The legal rules in the Qur'ān are limited and relatively very few indeed, if we compare these rules to the total number of verses in the Qur'ān. While the total number of verses in the Qur'ān is about 6,236, the verses that have to do with legal matters represent only a small portion of that, about two hundred verses in all, of which many have been abrogated. These verses generally deal with personal status and inheritance law.

(6) Militants believe that jihād or holy war is an absolute religious duty.

Since the militants believe wrongly that Muhammad's path and message have abrogated any other paths (say, Christianity and Judaism), they maintain that jihād means to impose Islam on the infidels at any time and anywhere, to convert them to the right path and the true faith. Islamic regions are considered abodes of peace (*Dār al-Islām*), while the rest of the world is declared abodes of war (*Dār al-Harb*). The militants believe that the two zones will be in permanent confrontation until non-Muslims are converted to Islam.

Initially, the term *jihād* in the Qur'ān and in the prophetic traditions meant self-control and self-refinement. In fact, this meaning of the word was called by the Prophet "the great jihād." In terms of war, jihād is only to be used as an act of self-defense. If interpreted as more than this, it is not jihād but aggression, forbidden by the verses and the very spirit of the

Qur'ān. Jihād is not a pillar of Islam. The one-sided stress placed on holy wars and fighting is a historical distortion of the real concept of jihād and is due to political interests.

(7) Militants are known for their efforts to push for religious segregation and sectarian strife.

Militants believe that each person should stay in his or her own community and forbid interrelationships between Muslims and non-Muslims. The reason for this is again wrong interpretation of the Qur'ān. When the Qur'ān stated that Muslims have no relationship with non-Muslims, it was necessitated by a temporary situation (the war between the Prophet and the Jews in Medina). That situation, eventually, no longer existed. The permanent rule in the Qur'ān is to have an attitude of good relationship with non-Muslims. Moreover, the Qur'ān allows Muslims to marry non-Muslim women (from among the People of the Book). A son or daughter born of such a marriage would naturally have a mixture of Muslim and non-Muslim uncles and aunts. Cutting off relationships and instilling enmity into people because of their difference in faith is considered, in true Islam, inhuman.

These are the main characteristics of the militant doctrine and the liberal movement's response to it. It goes without saying that militant doctrine not only poses a danger and a threat to humanity, to peace and civilization, but also undermines Islam itself, falsifying its great teachings, terminating its vital spirit and putting an end to its humane attitudes.

Jihād or Holy War in Islam

Jihād is the most sensitive word in the Islamic vocabulary. It is always used, heard and understood in a very emotional way, either positive or negative. To non-Muslims, jihād is a holy war against them, a raised sword not easily sheathed. To many Muslims, jihād is the religious duty to guide non-Muslim peoples to the right and true faith. Militants believe jihād is a divine precept to impose Islam, the ultimate faith, on non-Mus-

lims. Only a minority of Muslims live jihād's moral and spiritual meaning.

The literal meaning of the Arabic word *jihād* is striving, contention or
struggle. Jihād, then, has many meanings: obstinate opposition or resistance; contending resolutely with a task or a problem; strenuous efforts
toward an end; doing something difficult; a strong effort, or series of
efforts, against any adverse agencies or conditions, in order to maintain
one's existence or manner of life.

In the initial Meccan phase of the Qur'ānic revelation (610–622 C.E.) the
word *jihād* was used in an ethical, moral and spiritual sense. Initially,
jihād meant to maintain one's faith and serenity in the midst of adverse
conditions. In the Meccan period the Prophet was told through revelation to be patient with the Meccans, to suffer quietly, and not meet force
with force: "Remind them [the people of Mecca], for thou art but a re-
membrance, Thou art not at all a dominator over them" (Sūra 88:22). "But
be patient [Muhammad] with a patience fair to see" (Sūra 70:5). "Say [it
is] truth from the Lord of you [all]. Then whosoever will, let him believe,
and whosoever will, let him disbelieve" (Sūra 29:18). And to the Muslim
community as a whole, the Prophet recited: "Exhort one another to truth
and exhort one another to endurance" (Sūra 103:3).

Then how did jihād come to mean holy war? In the Medinan phase of
the Qur'ānic revelation (622–632 C.E.), the word *jihād* came to include the
struggle of the individual or the community with the Meccans: "We have
enjoined on man kindness to parents, but if they strive to make thee join
with me [God] that of which thou hast no knowledge, then obey them
not" (Sūra 29:8). It is also written: "As for those who strive in us [God], we
surely guide them to our paths" (Sūra 29:69). "So obey not the unbelievers, but strive against them with a real endeavor" (Sūra 25:52).

The Meccans continued to persecute the new Muslim community. The
Prophet and the new Muslim community were forced to migrate to Medina, about five hundred kilometers to the north, in the historic flight
called the *hijra*. They left their homeland, families, trades and fortunes.
The Qur'ān in its Medinan verses states: "The true believers are those

only who believe in God [Allah] and his messenger [Muhammad], and afterward doubt not, but strive with their wealth and their lives for the cause of the God [Allah]. Such are the sincere" (Sūra 49:15). "But the Messenger and those who believe with him, strive with their wealth and their lives" (Sūra 9:388).

Because of the circumstances of the period, the initial spiritual meaning of jihād, striving and struggle, gave ground to the new material meaning, to struggle together against the evil and harmful aggression of the people of Mecca. Eventually, the material meaning came to dominate the spiritual meaning. Muslims threatened Meccan caravans coming from Syria and occasionally attacked them in order to force the Meccans to recognize the new Muslim community and to allow Muslims to visit Mecca where their families, possessions and memories remained. Mecca to them—and to all Muslims—has a great significance; it is the axis of Islam. In Mecca is found the *Kaʿba* (a small stone building said to be initially built by Abraham and Ishmael). The pilgrimage is made to the Kaʿba and other prescribed places in Mecca.

Still the Meccans kept up their resistance against the new Muslims. The Meccans prepared an army of a thousand men to fight three hundred Muslims. They went to the north to exterminate the Muslims in 624 C.E. Jihād took on a new meaning in its second manifestation; it came to mean a holy war. However, the Qurʾānic verses also stipulate the conditions and limits of fighting: "Sanction is given unto those who fight because they have been wronged, and God [Allah] is indeed able to give them victory. Those who have been driven from their homes unjustly, only because they said, Our Lord is God [Allah]" (Sūra 22:29). "Fight in this way of God [Allah] against those who fight against you, but begin not hostilities. So, God [Allah] loveth not aggressors" (Sūra 2:190). Thus, jihād, as holy war, according to the Qurʾānic definition, is a war satisfying certain stringent conditions, with a particular cause, well-defined enemies, strict limits to the fighting and particular ethical rules for its conduct. The chief ethical rule is that Muslims are not to be aggressors or to initiate hostilities.

The real first battle between Muslims and Meccans, the battle of Badr (624 C.E.), was won by the Muslims. On their way back to Medina, the Prophet said to them: "We (the Muslims) have turned from the minor jihād to the major one [struggle]." Clearly the Prophet saw the battle of Badr for what it was: minor jihād. The more important and more difficult struggle continued—ethical, moral and spiritual jihād. This jihād is a strenuous effort, or series of efforts, to discipline oneself against greed, avarice, cowardice, fear, tyranny, ignorance, submission to negative elements, yielding to evil desires and giving way to passion. This jihād avoids a meaningless existence and an empty, if not easy and comfortable, life. This is the major jihād. While armed conflict and warfare may be associated with jihād, jihād is much more than physical force or holy war.

Later, in 626 C.E., a segment of the Jewish community (the Bani Qurayza tribe of Medina) renounced their agreed upon allegiance with the Muslims. At this time the Muslims were close to being defeated by the Meccans. A verse was revealed commanding the Muslims to protect Islam by fighting the Jewish covenant breakers: "Fight against such of those who have been given the Scripture [People of the Book] as believe not in God [Allah] nor the last day, and forbid not that which God [Allah] hath forbidden by his Messenger, and follow not the faith of truth, until they pay the tribute readily" (Sūra 9:29). Because this Jewish tribe betrayed the Muslims and renounced their allegiance to them, the tribe was considered unfaithful to their own faith, or apostates. It is very clear from this verse that to fight against the People of the Book is conditional and not general or absolute. Moreover, the Qur'ān says nothing of converting the People of the Book to Islam or of eliminating them. In fact, the Qur'ān warns: "Forbid not that which has not been forbidden by the messenger [Muhammad]."

Thus, in its third manifestation, jihād came to mean to fight those who believe not in God or the Last Day and to force them to pay a tribute as a sign of their surrender to the Muslim community. The concept of tribute was applied to the People of the Book—Christians or Jews—living in the

Muslim community. The tribute was a substitute for becoming a soldier, since non-Muslims could not fight in the Muslim army. The tribute was a tax to be collected by the state as a subsidy to the army from those unable or not allowed to fight.

In its fourth manifestation, after the conquest of Mecca (630 C.E.), the meaning of jihād or holy war came to include the coercion of all Meccans to Islam. All Meccans were to confess that God is one God, and that the Prophet Muhammad is his messenger (Sūra 2 and Sūra 9). Hence, the meaning of jihād was the conversion of non-Muslims to Islam.

To summarize: Jihād is always major, as the Prophet stated, when one fights the negative elements in oneself in order to grow in serenity and strength. Jihād as warfare is just the minor jihād, not to be confused with or compared to the major jihād. The major jihād implies self-improvement and legitimate self-defense. Many scholars who have influenced the thinking of Muslims believe that jihād is always a war against non-Muslims. They believe that this war will continue until Islam becomes the sole faith of all peoples of the world. War, then, becomes a permanent attitude. This understanding of jihād is a grave departure from its original meaning.

Emphasis on armed aggression results from the wrong use of a Qur'-ānic verse and two prophetic traditions: "O ye who believe: Fight those of the disbelievers who are close to you" (Sūra 9:123). On closer examination, this verse is not to fight all unbelievers (non-Muslims who do not believe in the Prophet Muhammad and his message) in every place and at all times; rather it has a strategic meaning—to fight only the unbelievers who are living geographically close to the Muslim community. Its emphasis is on self-defense and on the security of the community. Application of this verse can be seen in an action taken by the Prophet just before his death. In 632 C.E. the Prophet prepared an army to invade his enemies to the north. The Muslim community was surrounded by mighty and powerful enemies, the Roman Empire to the north and the Persian Empire to the east. At that time, attacking these enemies was the best strategy for the defense of the new Muslim community.

There are also two prophetic traditions from the Ḥadīth that have been misused and that distort the true meaning of jihād. It is said that before the Prophet's migration, he was provoked by the Meccans and said to them: "I came to you with slaughter. I was ordered (by the revelation) to fight the people until they say: there is no God but God (Allah), and Muhammad is his messenger, and to pray and to give alms" (from the sayings of the Prophet, the Ḥadīth).

It is not historically certain that the Prophet actually said to the Meccans, "I came to you with slaughter." If that really happened, it might have been said by the Prophet in anger. It did occur that the Prophet—in a moment of anger—promised after the battle of Uhud (625 C.E.) to kill double the number of Muslims killed and to disfigure and deform the Meccans as much as he could, more than they had done to the Muslims. However, a Qur'ānic verse (Sūra 2:190) was revealed, ordering him not to do this and to dispense retribution (one for one, injury for injury). Had the Prophet said this about slaughter—which is doubtful—these verses reveal that he was wrong to have spoken so. The Qur'ān ranks higher than the oral traditions (Ḥadīth), and if there is any contradiction, that which is written in the Qur'ān should have precedence in interpretation and application.

As for the second prophetic tradition that was distorted, many interpreters say that the word *people* in the Qur'āan does not mean all the people at every time and in every place, but rather the people of Mecca at the time of the revelation. Because of this, the prophetic tradition that the Prophet was ordered to fight "the people" until they say, "There is no deity but God and Muhammad is his messenger," is in perfect harmony with the verses of the Qur'ān ordering the Muslims to fight the Meccans of that time until they declare they are Muslims. There is no contradiction at all between the Qur'ānic verse and the prophetic tradition. The apparent contradiction is due to the misinterpretation of the tradition.

Fighting nearby enemies began in Islam as a strategy to protect the Muslim community from the two major empires of that time (the Roman and the Persian). Fighting nearby enemies lost its defensive character and became more political in nature after the period of the four rightly guided Caliphs and when the Islamic state had become an empire (about 660 C.E.).

ʿUmar, the second Caliph (634–644 C.E.), hesitated to invade either the Roman or the Persian empire. Finally, he was obliged to do so to protect Islam and the Muslim community. The word *jihād* was then used according to its true meaning.

Less than one generation (twenty-eight years) after the death of the Prophet, the government in Islam had become an empire in which the Caliphate had become hereditary and the Caliph had become a de facto emperor. The Caliphate emperors invaded other countries to gain more power, more wealth, more subjects or to protect what they had gained. The Caliphate emperors and their jurists aroused and excited the people by the use of the word *jihād*, thus implying that they were invading under the flag of Islam and in God's name to give Islam more power and to guide other people to the truth. The question, however, is one of principle. Muslim conquerors invaded foreign countries for temporal purposes and earthly concerns under the flag of the faith and in the name of God, calling it jihād. Some believe that the Caliphs' wars were basically to spread Islam. Perhaps there was some thought along these lines, but for the most part, wars were fought for the benefit of the Caliphs themselves, their families and their courts.

Another meaning was given to jihād by dissidents within the empire. Those opposed to the Caliphs would define their opposition to the Caliphs' actions as jihād. They believed that jihād is not only against unbelievers but also against unjust rulers.

A third meaning was fabricated by fanatics and terrorists. These groups mean by jihād the murder of those opposed to their views.

The meaning of jihād is confused in Muslim minds, a result of incorrect usage of the word through most of Islamic history. Many do not know or critically examine the authentic meaning.

In sum, jihād has dual meanings: its religious meaning and its historically determined political meaning. In its authentic religious meaning, jihād is a strong effort or series of efforts against negative behavior or unjust conditions in order to keep one's faith strong and one's existence stable and open to progress; it is to instill justice and mercy in one's conscience and then to establish justice and mercy in the community through the individual and the collective conscience. In its historically determined political meaning, jihād is self-defense and nothing more. It is not aggression, hostility or confrontation. It is unfortunate that the misunderstanding of jihād has become so prevalent. Jihād is mercy, not a sword; and justice, not violence. And Islam is not a state for some people but a path of mercy for all people; not an empire for powerful rulers, but a faith for humankind.

Reforming Islam and Law

Despite the fact that Islam dawned in a desert environment, it carried the potential to create a vast civilization. When the Arabs conquered Persia, Syria and Egypt in the first century of Islam, they were faced with well-established civilizations and superpowers of the day. The Arabs lost no time in selecting the most pertinent endowments of each civilization for the new civilization they intended to establish. In time, Islam itself became a well-established civilization, spreading across most of the Middle East. This civilization respected ethics and humanity.

Over the centuries a variety of schools were founded propounding various legal rules, theologies and philosophies. Unfortunately, their debates often raged over minor matters that were difficult to prove. The *mū'atazīla*, or withdrawers, thought rationally but stressed that the Qur'ān is created and not eternal. Opposing the mū'atazīla were the traditionalists, who deemed the Qur'ān eternal and uncreated. Had the debate centered on the historical context of the Qur'ān, the debate would have been profitable and effective. Instead, the debate moved from the philosophical sphere into the political sphere. Under Caliph Ma'amun (813–833 C.E. / 198–218 A.H.), the mū'atazīla came to power. Despite their advocacy of rationalism, they sought to impose their doctrine with the backing of state force.

A few years later, the mūʿatazīla were ousted from power and were replaced by the traditionalists. Wary of the mūʿatazīla, the traditionalists judged reason and the mind dangerous, liable to arouse strange ideas to be applied with force. Led by theologians Ashaari (873–941 C.E.) and Al-Ghazzali (1059–1111 C.E./606 A.H.) the traditionalists argued that since God is omnipotent and ruler over all, the mind, reason and causality could effect nothing and man's actions are acts of God not of the individual. Al-Ghazzali added that there was only one causality—that of God. Fire is not caused by striking a match, nor wetness by throwing water. Both fire and water are the products of the will of God. Thus, everything is owned by God, and man, reason and causality are active agents; they are mere illusions to delude mankind.

Al-Ghazzali set down his ideas in his book *The Revival of Religious Sciences,* in which he classified all human activities in chapters replete with citations from fabricated prophetic traditions. Al-Ghazzali's book was deemed the core of Islam and not a book written by man, despite its reliance on fabrication. With the loss of causality and free will, the Islamic mind closed, and Islam lost its vitality and potential for development. Thereafter, Islam, as a philosophical system, slipped into degeneration.

Two hundred years ago Muslims were rudely awakened by European enlightenment. With the French invasion of Egypt in 1798–1800 C.E., Egypt, and later the rest of the Middle East, felt the shock of Western civilization. Egypt led in the renewal of spirit and mind. Egyptian youth were dispatched to the universities of Europe. Egyptian confidence and knowhow returned, and soon Egypt felt competent to rule in place of the Western powers that occupied its land. In Egypt's battle for liberation, Western colonization was viewed by some people as a second round of the Crusades, sparking enmity against the West.

For the past three decades the West has been transformed into a global civilization, while the Islamic world has produced little or nothing at all. Paradoxically, many Muslims curse international civilization as a neo-Western invasion, yet surround themselves with Western technology (products, gadgets). Muslims, particularly those in the Gulf, indulged in

Western technology in a way that could have been a boon to Islamic power and mind but instead became its bane. The passive acquisition of technology or gadgets, dislocated from the science of production, monopolized Islamic activities without refining the mind. Even today, this lack of refinement besets the Islamic world. Electronic means of communication—from airplanes to faxes—have reduced the meaning of time and space, leaving only the unfilled vacuum of leisure.

Many Muslims have called for the reform of Islam, but differ about how to set about it. One proposal calls for a return to the Golden Age in which contact with international civilization is severed. This reform, however, provides no solution as to how to make do without lasers, airplanes and telephones. This proposal advocates blind faith, giving rise to a false feeling of peace.

A second proposal calls for the wholesale adoption of modern technology so that the Islamic world can be absorbed into international civilization. While the first proposal seeks to return the Islamic world to the ideas of Ashaari and Al-Ghazzali, the second proposal struggles to embrace the new reality of contemporary civilization.

A third proposal for reform, which I advocate, falls between the two extremes. This proposal calls for a revival of Islamic mind, ethics and human rights and an integration of these with contemporary civilization so that we can share effectively in developing civilization instead of merely consuming it. This reform calls for the abandonment of the Ashaari and Al-Ghazzali doctrine. Instead Muslims should respect causality and the potential of man, without which thinking, invention and science are void. Man, not God, must be made responsible for his works. This understanding places man in history. Religious ideas evolve, moving in time and space, through history and place.

In addition, this proposal cares deeply for human rights, even if the term was not coined by Islamic civilization. Human rights ensure that every Muslim may speak according to what he believes. Human rights ensure that every Muslim respect the human brotherhood and recognize that God is for all human beings—good and evil, believers and unbelievers. This proposal advocates employing the technology of civilization while integrating it with *true* Islamic values. The notion of participating in humanity's technological evolution and respecting human rights is slowly but surely taking root in the Islamic world. However, at the same time, its advocates have become a target for militants. Militants have created movements of terror across the Islamic world and have disseminated their practices abroad. By their misdeeds they have distorted the image of Islam, and isolated Muslims from history. Those who seek to adapt the Islamic world, to accommodate contemporary civilization, are attacked and intimidated into silence. Those, such as myself, who seek to grasp the technology of contemporary civilization and blend it with Islamic identity are also attacked and intimidated into silence.

The Islamic world has been torn between the liberals and the militants. Unfortunately, few Muslims have put forward strategies to heal the divisions. Meanwhile the world continues evolving apace, augmenting its capacities by the minute, leaving the vast morass of Muslims to detach themselves from time and space by their behavior, moving nowhere but backward. Muslims opt not for sharing, but for resisting civilization, opposing its forces and consuming its products, then reacting to this consumption by violence against themselves, their society and the world. In addition, Islamic religious institutions operate de facto and religious officials defend their wealth and align themselves with militants and reactionaries against progress.

Moreover, in Egypt, the moderates and enlightened are subject to punishment by the nation's legislation. Under Article 98(f) of the penal code, it states, "Whosoever writes against the deity or vilifies it or any of its sects, should be imprisoned for no less than six months and no more than five years, or be fined E£500." Militant Muslims, who include religious authorities, have implored the government to bring the moderates and enlightened to trial charged with infringement of Article 98. Since religious officials hold that they are the sole legitimate representatives of Islam, they consider any vilification of themselves to be a vilification of Islam. Thus, they call on the government to apply the article on all who preach or write against their closed and narrow-minded instructions.

Similarly Article 161 of the penal code punishes with imprisonment for three years and a fine ranging from E£100 to E£500 all who publish anything judged against any faith accepted in Egypt. Islam, Christianity and Judaism are all faiths accepted in Egypt but only militant Muslims turn to Article 161 to punish their opponents. Militant Muslims see the moderates and enlightened as assaulting Islam itself rather than seeking its reform. In most of the Islamic world, the situation has become critical. Without an Islamic reformation—renewal of the Islamic mind, ethical code and respect for human rights—Muslims will be excluded from the international community and be severed from its time and history. Articles 98 and 161 must be annulled from Egyptian law. Legal license for militants and religious officials to intimidate intellectuals in the Muslim world must be curtailed. The way should be cleared for reformists to express their ideas through the media and press without intimidation, threat or prosecution. Without this, I fear for the future of Islam and humanity.

Islamic Law and Human Rights

Human rights, the expression and the concept, were never known during the medieval period when Islamic law was first established. Human rights, as a claim by any person, such as the right to worship as one chooses, the right to free speech, etc., were initially declared during the French Revolution (1789 c.e.). In time, the concept became widely accepted, especially when the human race suffered from the denial of human rights by totalitarian governments, fascistic parties, misleading media and tyranny in general. Today, human rights constitute an international call and a humanitarian creed to liberate people from any fear or tyranny, to free our capacities from any obstacles so that we may live in peace, spread peace and interrelate with the community, humanity and the cosmos.

It is necessary to realize that Muslims have neither one unified attitude toward Islamic law nor one clear understanding about human rights. Actually, in the Islamic world today, there are two movements, each one with its own understanding of Islamic law and human rights. As previously discussed, the first is fanatical, extremist and militant; the second is liberal, intellectual and enlightened.

The first movement, namely the fanatical, extremist, militant, believes that Islamic rights are primary to human rights. What are Islamic rights? It is a question answered only by the fanatics, the extremist and the militants, and specifically defined and detailed by their leaders, who believe they monopolize the truth and are entitled by God to impose the truth forcefully, even by the sword in jihād or holy war. They believe that Islamic law is revealed from God, without making any distinction between Islamic law and Islamic jurisprudence. God, they say, knows humankind and society better than man, and God revealed Islamic law to be enforced upon man for his own benefit and that of society. This movement argues that applying Islamic law strictly would refine society, instill justice and spread prosperity. They believe that neither humanity nor society has the right to legislate themselves. Laws were already legislated by God in the Qurʾān for all human beings, anytime and in every place.

Democracy is thought to be a Western system, not Islamic, according to this movement, and is considered heresy. The Islamic political system is based on *shūra* (consultation), which means that the ruler (the Caliph or the Imam) has the right to appoint counselors to offer advice when he wants it. However, he is not obliged to take their advice, even if there is consensus among them. His decision is seen as infallible, whether de jure (in the Shīʿite doctrine) or de facto (in the Sunnite doctrine). To the fanatical, extremist militant movement, humanity has no right to choose their own faith, unless they are non-Muslims and convert to Islam. And Muslims have no right to convert from Islam or else they will be subject to the death penalty.

This movement believes that no one has the right to free opinion or free speech. They believe that Muslims should mold themselves according to the traditions of their sect or community or group. They are to suppress their opinions and bond themselves to the community. Any different opinion expressed is considered an act against God and against the community. Such a person is considered to be at war with God and the community; thus, subject to the death penalty or to being murdered by any Muslim.

This movement believes that non-Muslims living in an Islamic country are obliged to behave the same as a Muslim and not to act, speak or declare a viewpoint that might be considered against Islam or Islamic traditions or the Islamic community. As part of the minority, non-Muslims have to obey the majority. And in non-Islamic countries, the majority—non-Muslims—are to behave toward minority Muslims as if Muslims were in an Islamic country, otherwise the fanatic, extremist militants claim discrimination.

This movement believes women are under the custody of a man, whether he be her father, brother, husband or son. A woman has no right to leave the house without permission from her custodian. If she is married, she has no right to work unless she has her husband's permission and then only in certain jobs, such as teaching girls, caring for women, and the like. A woman has no right to wear what she wants. She must don the veil or the *chadoor* (in Iran), and if she does not, she could be considered a heretic, which is punishable by death (as was declared in Iran). A woman has no right to drive a car, and if she does, she will be considered a rebel against the community, endangering herself and her husband, which happened in Saudi Arabia.

The liberal, intellectual, enlightened movement has another approach and totally different concepts and ideas about Islamic law and human rights. To this movement, human rights never contradict Islamic law. This movement stresses that there is a distinction between Islamic law and Islamic jurisprudence.

This movement believes that not all the legal rules mentioned in the Qurʾān are permanent, that some of them are temporary. A very specific example is slavery and slavery harems. Slavery and slave harems were mentioned in the Qurʾān; as previously cited, they were not abrogated, yet they are not applied today and are forbidden by law. Even though the principle was not clear to him and to the Muslims of his time, the second Caliph, ʿUmar, stopped applying certain rules from the Qurʾān.

This movement believes that everyone has a share in political life. Public discussions and laws should be implemented only after extensive discussion and an open and free process of voting. Democracy is a must at every level and in every unit of society.

This movement believes that political actions are mere civil actions, not religious actions. The head of the state, ministers (state secretaries), governors and all other civil servants are not infallible. Their acts can be criticized and even canceled, if necessary.

This movement believes that all people have the right to choose their own faith without being threatened by the death penalty. Verses stating freedom of choosing one's faith have not been and never were abrogated from the Qurʾān. According to the Qurʾān, forcing someone to be or to become a Muslim against his will is distorting the meaning and the spirit of Islam and is a denial of human rights. Islam has no need for hypocrites or oppressed nonfree people.

This movement believes that everyone has the right to free speech and to express ideas and opinions the way he or she chooses. If these opinions prove to be correct, they will benefit all the community; if not, they should be debated decently and not suppressed by any means.

Finally, this movement believes that men and women have equal rights—the right to free speech, the right to work, and to drive a car. Women should never be under the custody of anyone. If humanity has obligations to God, it also has rights. Humanity's first and major right is to be free, with free mind and free conscience, rather than enslaved by anyone, any political power, any religious group or any false media.

To the liberal, intellectual, enlightened movement, jihād is self-control. If jihād is applied to war, it should only be applied for self-defense. To the liberal, intellectual, enlightened movement, each human being is a word of God and is entitled to every human right. To this movement, justice precedes punishment, the spirit is more important than the text and humanity is one community.

Glossary

Adonay (Hebrew): When Judaism came into being in the work of Moses, the Egyptian word *Aten* became the Hebrew word *Adonay,* meaning the God.

Amen (Ancient Egyptian): Temporal name, function or attribute of the one and only God who is with no second, associate or partner.

Amr (Arabic): Conduct of affairs, authority, command, etc.

ankh (Ancient Egyptian): (♀); the symbol of life in ancient Egypt.

Aten (Ancient Egyptian): A temporal name, function, or attribute of the one and only God who is with no second, associate or partner. In the time of Akhenaton, it was the power behind the sun; the ultimate God.

Awlīya (Arabic): Friends of God or holy men.

Al-Azhar Mosque and Al-Azhar University: The oldest and the premier university of Islamic studies, in Cairo (Jami'at al-Azhar).

Caliph or Khalīfa (English, Arabic): A successor of Muhammad as temporal and de facto a spiritual head of Islam.

Dār al-Islām/Dār al-Harb (Arabic): The "place of peace," where the religion of Islam prevails, as contrasted with the "place of war," where non-Muslims predominate; used in the context of external jihād.

Egyptian Book of the Dead: The Egyptians used to put all the sacred texts in a papyrus (or a book) with the deceased. It was called *per em hru*, which means "manifested in light," and is actually known as *The Egyptian Book of the Dead*.

Elohīm (Hebrew): Many gods.

al-fiqh (Arabic): Religious law, Islamic jurisprudence.

hadd (plural hūdūd) (Arabic): A determined punishment; "to the limits" (full limits of the law), such as stoning for adultery or cutting of the hands of thieves.

Hammurabi's Law: In effect from 1792 to 1750 B.C.E. A set of laws put into the Old Testament as a way of replacing conscience (or the Egyptian Ma'at) with legal rules.

hieroglyphics: The holy writings of the ancient Egyptian priesthood.

hijāb (Arabic): Covering; used in reference to Islamic-style dress increasingly adopted by women in the Arab-Islamic world, such as *chadoor*; also refers to religious amulets that contain ("cover") sacred texts.

hōkum (Arabic): To judge; justice administration.

hokhma (Hebrew): Wisdom; God created the world through wisdom.

Horus: The Egyptian god of light and the son of Osiris and Isis.

'Id al-Fitr (Arabic): Holiday ending the month of fasting, Ramadan.

Imam (Arabic): Prayer leader of a mosque; a Muslim leader of the line of 'Ali held by Shī'ites to the divinely appointed, sinless, infallible successors of Muhammad; any of various rulers who claim descent from Muhammad and exercise spiritual and temporal leadership over a Muslim region.

Islam: The peace that comes from submission to the one God, Allah; the last of the great prophetic traditions traceable to Abraham.

jihād (Arabic): Struggle or great effort of Muslims, which can be either internal, as in the struggle within oneself to live an upright life, or external, as in the better-known "holy war" to defend the religion.

Kāʿba (Arabic): A small stone building in the court of the Great Mosque at Mecca that contains a sacred black stone, the focal point of Muslim prayer.

kāfirūn (Arabic): Unbelievers in Islam.

Kemal Ataturk: (1881–1938). Originally Mustafa Kemal. Turkish general and president of Turkey (1923–38). He abolished the caliphate.

Khalīfa (see Caliph)

Levite: A member of the priestly Hebrew tribe of Levi; a Levite of non-Aaronic descent assigned to lesser ceremonial offices under the Levitical priests of the family of Aaron.

Maʾat (Ancient Egyptian): Conscience. The Egyptian goddess of Truth, she is the expression of the cosmos and the individual conscience; the true way and the real law of conduct. Osiris was the Lord of Maʾat, which referred to righteousness, justice, upright living and order.

Muftī (Arabic): One who opens the way; one with legitimate authority to issue an official religious opinion, or fatwa; also the official title of a highest religious leader, as the Muftī of Egypt.

Neter: In the Hieroglyphic language, neter designates either the God or a god or gods.

Osiris: The Egyptian god of the underworld and husband and brother of Isis.

Qurʾān: The Holy Book of Islam composed of sacred revelations made to Muhammad by Allah through the angel Gabriel.

Quraysh: The prophet Muhammad's tribe in pre-Islamic Arabia; coming from the extended family or lineage of the Prophet.

Ra: The Egyptian sun god.

Rabbi (Hebrew): Used by Jews as a term of address; a Jew trained and ordained for professional religious leadership and the official leader of a Jewish congregation.

Ramadan: The ninth month of the Islamic year, observed with fasting (sawm) practiced daily from dawn to sunset.

Sabians: A sect who worship God and emphasize astrology and astronomy through the stars.

sadaqa (Arabic): Gift giving. Sadaqa is derived from the Hebrew word tzedeq, meaning righteousness.

al-Sadat, Anwar: Egyptian military and civil nationalist leader who succeeded Nasser and opened economic relations with the West and political relations with Israel; he was assassinated in 1981 by a militant Islamist group.

Set, Setan: The brother of Osiris. Set became Setan in the Canaanite language, then Hebrew, and Setan (Satan in English) became the personification of evil and the opponent of God.

Sharīʿa (Arabic): Path, method or way. Islamic law, as it has been interpreted by the religious scholars belonging to one of the four main schools of Islamic jurisprudence.

Shīʿa Islam: The branch of Islam traced to the historical dispute in the early decades after the introduction of the religion over the question of succession, whether the rightful caliph should be from the family of ʿAli, the Prophet's son-in-law, or from among the pious Muslims.

shūra (Arabic): Consultation; a method approximating democracy by which Islamic rulers should govern.

Sufism: Islamic mysticism, an Arabic form of the Greek word Safia, meaning wisdom. Many scholars think this term derives from the Arabic suf, meaning wool, but the author sees its origin as Greek.

Sunni Islam: The majority branch (90 percent) of the world's Muslim population, as contrasted with the miniority Shī'a branch of Islam.

Sūra (Arabic): A group of verses from the Qur'ān.

Talmud (Hebrew): The authoritative body of Jewish tradition comprising the Mishnah and Gemara and forming the basis of Judaism.

tā'zir (Arabic): Supporting or strengthening. For example, punishing the criminal is to support and strengthen the criminal to take the right path.

Thoth: The messenger of God, the Lord of divine words or Lord of the words of God. Thoth held the word of Osiris to be true, or "the word made true."

'Umar: The second caliph (634–644 C.E.)

'Usr (Ancient Egyptian): Mostly means strength, might, power. Another name for Osiris.

waqf (Arabic): Islamic religious bequest for a charitable purpose, such as the support of a mosque, school or hospital; cannot be altered or renegotiated once made.

Yahweh (Hebrew): Letters to allude to God, but is not His name. In time Yahweh was seen as God of the Hebrews.

zakāt (Arabic): Religiously inspired charitable donations, one of the five pillars of Islam; increasingly mandated as a tax as part of the drive toward Islamization of government.

Zohar: The Egyptian priests had some certain knowledge by which they could use numbers and letters to predict or foretell many things; some of this knowledge became the Jewish culture Zohar.